Families in Today's World

D0453805

Families in Today's World is an international textbook providing a quick introduction for students studying sociology of family in different countries around the world. It provides comprehensive coverage of the major topics in the sociology of family life.

Written in an easily accessible manner, the book opens with a chapter on defining family and family structures. It then moves on to discuss over a dozen major topics, from interaction and meaning in families to sexuality. David Cheal provides coverage of these topics by drawing on a variety of international material from countries around the world. Most of the studies focus on contemporary family life but Cheal also presents information on historical changes which have shaped family life as we know it today.

A prominent theme in the sociology of family today is diversity which makes this book an incredibly valuable teaching tool as it presents diversity in family patterns through thinking about family life globally. It is an essential resource for students of sociology, social policy, family studies and global issues.

David Cheal is a Professor of Sociology at the University of Winnipeg. His main areas of interest are Sociology Theory and the Sociology of the Family. He is the author of *Sociology of Family Life* (2002) and editor of *Family: Critical Concepts* (2003).

Families in Today's World

A comparative approach

David Cheal

Routledge
Taylor & Francis Group

LONDON AND NEW YORK

First published 2008
by Routledge
2 Park Square, Milton Park, Abingdon, Oxon OX14 4RN

Simultaneously published in the USA and Canada
by Routledge
270 Madison Avenue, New York, NY 10016

*Routledge is an imprint of the Taylor & Francis Group, an
informa business*

© 2008 David Cheal

Typeset in Sabon by
RefineCatch Limited, Bungay, Suffolk
Printed and bound in Great Britain by
CPI Antony Rowe, Chippenham, Wiltshire

British Library Cataloguing in Publication Data
A catalogue record for this book is available from the British Library

Library of Congress Cataloging in Publication Data
Cheal, David J.
Families in today's world: a comparative approach|David Cheal
p.cm.
1. Family. 2. Family–Cross-cultural studies. I. Title.
HQ519.C44 2007
306.85—dc 22   2007020405

ISBN 13: 978–0–415–35930–6 (pbk)
ISBN 13: 978–0–415–35931–3 (hbk)
ISBN 13: 978–0–203–00721–1 (ebk)
ISBN 10: 0–415–35930–-9 (pbk)
ISBN 10: 0–415–35931–7 (hbk)
ISBN 10: 0–203–00721–2 (ebk)

Contents

Preface

Families in Today's World is intended as an international textbook for students studying the sociology of the family in different countries. The key objective of this book is to cover the major topics in the sociology of the family revealed through a search of the literature. A second objective is to provide coverage of these topics by drawing on material from countries around the world. The book should be a valuable teaching tool because a prominent theme in the sociology of the family today is diversity, yet most family sociology textbooks study diversity only within national boundaries. *Families in Today's World* demonstrates diversity as a way of thinking about the family globally.

This book opens with a chapter on Defining Family and Family Structures. Problems in defining family are reviewed and different types of family are outlined. The dominance of the model of the nuclear family in earlier years is discussed, and described as the result of ideological assumptions about family life. Attention therefore shifts to describing social constructs of family life. It is concluded that because the concept of family refers to a wide range of diverse phenomena, it has no logical basis apart from the everyday usages of social actors. In the particular discourse of the social sciences, most of the categorizations of family life are types of family structures. The chapter then moves on to a description of family structures such as cohabitation, single-parent families, extended families and polygyny.

Chapter 2 takes up the subject matter of interaction and meaning in families. It is through their interactions that family members give meaning to their lives together, and define the expectations that one has of the other. This can be a particular problem where partners are emotionally together but are physically apart. Physical togetherness is easiest where family members share a home, and the chapter discusses the history of the home as a form of social organization. Home and family are seen by most people in modern societies as standing in opposition to the meanings of employment in the market economy, but how to express the strength of these bonds in the face of a dominant market economy is a practical problem. One way of doing this is through the ritualization of family ties, which is discussed next. Gift giving is described as a particularly important family ritual.

Social divisions are the subject of Chapter 3. One of the most prominent divisions involves gender differences. Special attention is paid to married women's economic dependency, which is inextricably linked to their place in a gender division of labour. Women's economic dependency is still strongly influenced by the primacy given to domestic and childcare work. The chapter then turns to racial divisions, and reviews the special characteristics of African-American families. Economic differences between families are discussed next, with a special emphasis given to the effects of low income. The chapter concludes with a discussion of the relationship between family income and family characteristics. Some types of families do very well economically, whereas others fare very poorly.

Chapter 4 focuses on social change. Major changes in family life are described, in both the Western societies and developing societies. If there is one master trend, it is that of individualization. Individuals have become differentiated from families and have acquired greater autonomy. Particular attention is paid to changing kinship ties in developing societies, and modernization theory is discussed. Divorce is discussed next, and the limitations of modernization theory are presented. Divorce rates have been changing everywhere, but they have not always been changing in the same direction. It is hypothesized that increases in women's employment and education in recent decades are responsible for several changes in family life, including increased divorce rates. Attention therefore shifts to a discussion of women and family change. Finally, the chapter ends with a section on the theory of the postmodern family.

The next chapter reviews the topic of demographic change. It opens by examining a common pattern of change in the Western societies and in some societies in Asia, namely falling birth rates. Reasons for declining fertility are analysed, and economic explanations and cultural explanations are presented. In economic explanations, the main focus is on the costs and benefits of having children. Cultural explanations of falling birth rates emphasize such factors as the declining influence of traditional norms, for example religious norms favouring large numbers of children. One of the consequences of declining fertility is population ageing, which is discussed next. This poses challenges for families and governments as they try to cope with the increasing numbers of elderly who are in need of support and care.

Chapter 6 discusses family, work and money. It begins with the topic of the division of labour between paid and unpaid work, which continues to reflect gender roles. The gendered nature of household work is discussed, and an examination of employment and housework finds that the amount of housework done by husbands does not vary much according to whether their wives are employed or not. The fact that men have not substantially increased their time spent on domestic chores as women have become increasingly employed outside the home has made it difficult for employed women to integrate a career with motherhood. Part-time employment is one strategy that many women have adopted to help them balance the need for earned income with family responsibilities. This chapter concludes with discussions of the economic position of single mothers, and the challenges of balancing work and family.

The next topic is caring, discussed in Chapter 7. Motivations to care are considered. Sometimes commitments to care arise from local norms about family relationships, and sometimes they arise from the dynamics of personal relationships. The relation between paid employment and private care is described. Providing care may affect participation in paid employment, but equally a potential carer's employment status may affect the likelihood of their becoming a carer and the nature of the care that is provided. Caregiving sometimes gives rise to tensions. For example, tensions may arise from a contradiction between a daughter feeling an obligation to provide care for an elderly parent and not wanting to let the caregiving role take over her life. Much caregiving is provided to elderly parents, but the elderly can be caregivers themselves. The contributions of older people are therefore described.

Chapter 8 takes up the subject of violence and sexual abuse. One hidden dimension of violence and sexual abuse towards females is the case of marital rape. Forced sex within marriage is only part of the oppression exercised against women and female children. Another aspect is forced marriage, affecting girls in particular, which is found in some countries and communities. Another risk faced by females is premature death. This is more a problem in some countries than in others, particularly where there is gender inequality in child mortality rates. In some countries there is higher female mortality than male mortality during early childhood, contrary to the usual pattern of higher male mortality than female mortality. Dowry-related violence is also an issue in some places, which is discussed next. The chapter concludes by reviewing information about wife beating. Forms of violence towards wives such as wife beating tend to be found in contexts where there is a strong patriarchal ideology which justifies male control over females.

The book then moves on to the topic of family formation in Chapter 9.

Three modes of family formation are discussed: marriage, moving in together and childbearing. Concerning marriage, the chapter focuses on age at marriage for women. The strongest and most consistent predictors of later age at marriage are women's education and their employment in non-agricultural activities. As a result of increases in female education and employment that occur with modernization, age at marriage for women has increased. Cohabitation is discussed next, and among other topics the antecedents of cohabitation are reviewed. Finally, the discussion reviews the debate about the relative importance of cultural factors versus economic factors in the causation of childbearing by single mothers.

Chapter 10 discusses parenting. The focus of this chapter is on the ways in which ideas about parenting, and childhood, have changed over time. The concept of intensive parenting is introduced as a historically constructed cultural model for appropriate childcare. In this model, parents assume a relatively great responsibility for the development of their children, and mothers in particular are seen as playing the preponderant role in shaping how their children will grow up. However, as more mothers are now employed outside the home, a new emphasis has emerged on involving fathers in child-rearing. Factors affecting fathers' involvement with their children are reported. The chapter ends with a discussion of contemporary conceptions of childhood and of the social relationships between children and parents.

Chapter 11 is concerned with family transformations, meaning the micro-sociological changes that occur during the lives of family members. Changes such as divorce or leaving home both have their impact on family life. In the last third of the twentieth century, divorce increased substantially in most developed nations. However, in some developing nations, notably in the Muslim world of Southeast Asia, divorce rates have actually fallen. Reasons for these patterns are presented. The consequences of divorce are discussed next, with a special focus on the disadvantages for children growing up in a single-mother family. The chapter concludes with a presentation of material on home leaving by young people. One of the sociological questions that has been examined about home leaving is whether it varies according to the history of family relationships and the social structure of the home that is being left. The available data suggest that there is a relationship between these factors.

In Chapter 12 we are reintroduced to the topic of kinship. The concept of the modified extended family is defined, and its relevance to contemporary family life is discussed. One of the noteworthy changes in the trend towards the modified extended family in Western societies has been a decline in co-residence between the generations. Nevertheless, despite physical separation, extended family ties are maintained. Outside the Western societies co-residence between extended kin is more common, and the extended family household is therefore described for selected Asian societies. Despite a general cultural preference for residential autonomy between the generations in the West, extended family living for instrumental reasons can also be found in Western societies. The idea that extended family households often function as safety nets for economically disadvantaged people is important.

Chapter 13 deals with family and state. The state often adopts a role as intervener in family life, either to meet family needs or for social control over families that are judged to be failing to meet their responsibilities. The first topic discussed is variations in welfare states which provide benefits and supports to families. Three types of welfare state are discussed, with examples, namely the social-democratic state, the corporatist state and the liberal state. Implications for families of these three regimes are outlined. Next, the chapter studies how the state uses the family as an instrument for policies to solve social problems. Examples are discussed where the state has devised policies to require parents to take more responsibility for their children and has promoted marriage as a way of reducing welfare dependency.

Finally, Chapter 14 takes up the topic of sexuality. Four issues are examined here. First, the chapter reviews evidence on changing attitudes towards premarital sexual behaviour. Generally, attitudes have become more permissive, although cultural differences persist. Second, the chapter discusses the challenges faced by lesbian mothers, and the strategies they adopt in response to them. The third section reports on the difficulties faced by women who work in the sex trade as they seek to maintain intimate relationships in the face of multiple sexual partners. And fourth, the problem of sexually transmitted disease is introduced with special reference to AIDS. In some parts of the world, notably in Sub-Saharan Africa, AIDS has become a scourge which has impacted upon family structure.

1 Defining family and family structures

Families are found everywhere, but what is family? Defining family has been a controversial topic. That is because different definitions have different implications for which social structures can legitimately lay claim to be recognized as families. To be recognized as living in a family is to have one's lifestyle socially validated and socially supported. Conversely, to live in a social arrangement that is not recognized as family is to occupy an ambiguous position in social life that runs the risk of being labelled as deviant (Bernardes, 1999).

The classic definition of the family was given by George Murdock, and we can begin there to see how difficult this issue has been (Murdock, 1960). Murdock defined the family as a social group characterized by common residence, economic cooperation, and reproduction. It includes adults of both sexes, at least two of whom maintain a socially approved sexual relationship, and one or more children, own or adopted, of the sexually cohabiting adults. This definition fits many people's experiences of family life, but not everyone's. In recent decades, understandings of family have been broadened to include a wider range of social structures.

Murdock's definition of the family states that the family is characterized by common residence. However, there are families in which one family member commutes regularly, or in which one or more family members spend extended periods of time elsewhere. What, then, should we make of married couples who live apart most of the time, and who maintain only visiting relationships with one another? Such relationships are found where husbands and wives are both committed to occupational careers that require them to live in different parts of the country, or even different parts of the world. They are also found in societies where economic opportunities are poor, and one of the partners (usually the husband) must migrate from a rural area to an urban area, or to another society, in order to earn a living for the family while the other partner (usually the wife) stays behind to bring up the children in their community of origin (Quddus, 1992). It is also the case that mothers sometimes live apart from their children but maintain economic and social relationships with them (Richter, 1996). Child fostering, particularly when women send their young children to grandparents in rural areas to be cared for, has been documented in many parts of the world.

Murdock's definition also states that the family is characterized by reproduction, and therefore includes children. However, childless couples have become increasingly prevalent in Western societies as fertility rates have fallen, and surely we would want to include these couples as families too. Finally, Murdock's definition states that the family consists of adults of both sexes. This restrictive definition would exclude single-parent families consisting of one adult plus her or his children. Such families have become increasingly prevalent as divorce rates increased. Once labelled as 'broken families', these social structures are widely recognized today as having the right to be recognized as families alongside families with two parents. More controversially, there are also social structures consisting of same-sex couples which have also made claims to be recognized as families. While there has been some resistance to extending the concept of family this far, same-sex couples have been increasingly successful in gaining social and legal recognition.

Restrictive as Murdock's definition was, his work did at least have the merit of recognizing that there is more than one type of family structure. Murdock stated that there are three types of families. The first type of family is the nuclear family. He said this family typically consists of a married man and woman and their offspring, although in some cases one or more additional persons may reside with them. According to Murdock, the nuclear family is a universal social grouping, either as the sole form of the family or as the basic unit from which more complex forms of family are constructed. The second type of family recognized by Murdock was the polygamous family. According to his definition, this type of family consists of two or more nuclear families that are affiliated because they have one married partner in common. Under polygyny, for instance, one man plays the role of husband and father in several nuclear families and thereby unites them into a larger familial group. Finally, the third type of family recognized by Murdock was the extended family. This consists of two or more nuclear families affiliated through an extension of the parent–child relationship. That is, the nuclear family of a married adult is joined to that of his or her parents.

Writing in the United States in the late 1950s, Murdock concluded that the nuclear family would be most familiar as the type of family recognized to the exclusion of all others by American society. Indeed, the nuclear family was prevalent in the 1950s, and for statistical purposes it was often regarded as the normal type of family. Martha Hill, writing in the USA in the mid-1990s, stated that the model family for designing social policy has been a co-resident nuclear unit with the husband-father as the main breadwinner and death as a prominent reason for losing the main breadwinner (Hill, 1995). In terms of family structure, the key assumption has been that a family is a nuclear family, consisting of a co-resident husband, wife, and (young) children. She concludes that this model has become unrealistic, and it should be considered as *a* model rather than *the* model of family.

Hill finds that the model of a co-resident nuclear family does not fit most age groups of adults. The co-resident nuclear family is the modal family situation of US children, but it does not characterize the family situation of about one quarter of them. Sharply rising divorce rates, plus large increases in births to unmarried mothers since the 1960s, make the single-parent household a prominent living arrangement for children. One in eight children is also growing up spending at least some time in an extended household, for example with grandparents or with aunts and uncles. The model of a co-resident nuclear family is an even poorer characterization of the family situation of adults. Adults are not normally in a co-resident nuclear family. Only among those aged 30–39 is the norm to be in a nuclear family with all children living together under one roof. Adults aged 50 or older are rarely in a co-resident nuclear family. In fact, for elderly persons an important living arrangement to take into account is living alone.

Furthermore, Hill points out that not all individuals related by descent, adoption or marriage live together in the same household. Major family ties are unobserved when only the relatives in the household are identified, an approach taken in many surveys and public programmes. Most official surveys are based on the household as the unit of analysis, using definitions of family that derive more from living arrangements than kinship ties. This approach can produce an incomplete accounting of relationships with family members living elsewhere. These relationships not only have emotional significance, but can also have material significance in such things as social support in times of ill-health or financial support in times of need. They are also relevant to the support of children by non-custodial parents, which has become increasingly important due to high rates of divorce and an increasing proportion of births occurring out of wedlock. Sizable segments of men in their 30s and 40s have young children living elsewhere and, hence, obligations that reach outside the nuclear family. On the other side, many young children live apart from one of their parents, but receive support, occasional or regular, from the absent parent. Of course, once they reach adulthood, most children live apart from their parents. Family ties therefore span more than one nuclear family, and many family transactions occur between nuclear families. The structure of link-ages connecting non-resident family members has received considerably less attention than co-resident family structures, despite their potential importance.

Similarly, Bernardes, writing in England, has noted that traditional family sociology has adopted a central ideal-type model of a presumed dominant nuclear family (Bernardes, 1985). The reality, he concludes, is one of variation and diversity. He goes on to argue that the traditional family model of the married heterosexual couple with children is part of a family ideology used by influential sections of society, such as the major religious organizations, in forming their own opinions and moral evaluations of family life. The divergence between this ideology and practical experiences of family life has become more open in recent years, as other sections of society have contested the previously domin-ant conceptualization of family life. Groups such as single mothers by choice, feminists and gays and lesbians have articulated challenges to the nuclear family model, and their voices have increasingly been heard. For example, the flagship journal of the National Council on Family Relations in the United States used to be called the *Journal of Marriage and the Family*. It is now called the *Journal of Marriage and Family*, reflecting the idea that there is no longer one dominant model of The Family but a diversity of patterns for family living. This changing viewpoint has reflected recent trends: an overall decline in husband–wife households, with attendant increases in female-headed households, people living alone, and unmarried women and men living together. In addition, the living arrangements of lesbians and gay men have become more visible. As perceptions have changed, so too awareness has grown that not only is there great variation in family structures but our pictures of family structures have been influenced by family ideologies.

Once we begin to view The Family as an ideological unit and recognize it as a moral statement, we can begin to unravel the complex process through which family relationships and The Family as a construct were mutually formed. For example, we can examine how social groups and state institutions have acted to define appropriate social behaviour. Ideologies affect how people behave, and they can be manipulated to produce outcomes favoured by those who possess relatively great social power.

FAMILY CONSTRUCTS

An ideology is a system of beliefs and values that defines social reality. It structures how we see the world and the conclusions that are drawn about appropriate lines of action. Family ideology ensures that certain parts of everyday family life are seen in a certain way, and that other elements of family lives are not seen at all. Ideologies gloss over the diversity, complexity and contradictions in relationships in favour of a unified construct of how the world is thought to really work. One such ideology is that of the nuclear family. This approach defines the nuclear family as the natural basis for family life (Bernardes, 1999). It claims that the nuclear family is a universal social institution that is the basic unit of society, and it recommends policies that encourage the formation of nuclear families. The modern nuclear family with a particular sexual division of labour has been writ large as The Family and elevated as the only desirable and legitimate family form.

Feminists have been especially concerned about the way in which this ideology has often been implicated in ideological definitions about natural gender differences in family life. For example, mothers rather than fathers have been seen as the natural caregivers for children, especially small children. Feminists have challenged ideological assumptions about the family (Thorne, 1982). They have argued against the ideology of the monolithic model of the family, which stresses the nuclear family with a breadwinner husband and a full-time wife and mother as the only natural and legitimate family form (Eichler, 1981). It is claimed that the monolithic model of the family leads to an unwarranted assumption of congruence between specific features of family life which vary in practice. This assumption of congruence generates bias in the data collection process and an inappropriate identification of what constitutes problem families. Feminists have challenged beliefs that any specific family arrangement is natural and inevitable. It is argued that beliefs that most people live in the nuclear family, that adult women usually have husbands to support them, and that motherhood is women's central vocation have legitimated the subordination of women. For example, lower wages for women have been justified by the assumption that their paid work is secondary to that of men. The belief that women are uniquely suited for domestic caregiving supports a sexual division of occupations in which women do jobs that resemble their roles as wives and mothers. And belief in the nuclear family justifies the idea that women depend upon the presence of a man. In short, the ideology of The Family reinforces women's domination by men.

Sometimes the family is conceived of more widely than the nuclear family in an ideology of familism. This is the case with policy discourses on family caregiving for the sick and the elderly. As the demand for care of the elderly in particular has risen, policy makers have articulated a vision of the family as the main provider of care. Here, the assumption is that there is a family consisting of a network of kin who are involved in providing care to a person in need (Keating *et al.*, 1994). Once again, a discourse of *the* family obscures real variations. Treating whole families as sources of support hides the extent to which social interactions shape the practical experiences of family life. There are two problems with such conceptualizations. First, not all close kin are involved in caregiving. For example, caregivers may have relatives whom they believe have obligations to help kin in need but who do not do so. Usually, only a certain proportion of any kinship network are actively involved in caring activities. However, the presumption that the family is (or should be) the main provider of care is part of the ideology of familism which holds that there is a kin group available for caregiving. The assumption that families provide care begs questions such as: which kin are actively supportive; which might be available to help but are not currently helping; which are unable or unwilling to help? The second problem with the ideology of familism in the policy discourse on family caregiving is that the structure of the caregiving family cannot be assumed by the presence or absence of kin, but it is socially constructed. Kin are included or excluded based on the preferences of the care recipients and the primary caregivers. Sometimes the preferred caregivers include non-kin who are close friends or neighbours of the primary caregiver or the care recipient. The caregiving family is not a monolithic entity determined by policy makers, but it is a socially constructed field of interactions with many variations. This includes such matters as the history of relationships, social expectations, and long-standing issues of affection or hostility. For example, the ways in which kin have interacted with one another in the past will set the stage for defining how much of the kinship network is included in the caregiving family.

If the caregiving family is socially constructed, it follows that different individuals may have quite different ideas on who comprises the family. These views may differ between ordinary people and social policy administrators, and among administrators themselves. For example, adult children may not recognize an obligation to help an ailing parent, because they are too busy, have jobs, or have other caregiving commitments. But social services administrators generally behave as if children are potential caregivers, often reducing or withholding services if there are children living locally, especially daughters. Social workers expect kin to help their elderly clients with a number of tasks, ranging from keeping in touch by phone to giving personal care. Or, to take another example, where financial benefits to caregivers are concerned, government regulations defining family for the purposes of administering social policy may exclude siblings even though some siblings provide care to one another in times of need such as ill-health.

The main conclusion to be drawn here is that 'family' is something that is socially constructed by particular groups of people in their interactions about the meanings of social relationships. The upshot is that so much variability has been revealed in what the family has been and is, that arriving at a single definition seems futile. Still, family has been and continues to be a meaningful category of human organization (Gubrium and Lynott, 1985). Because the concept of family refers to such a wide range of diverse phenomena, it has no logical basis apart from the everyday usages of social actors. A family is whatever people define it to be in their ongoing social interactions. This includes the definitions of actors in their everyday lives, as well as the definitions of social scientists who engage in formal discussions about family life. Social scientific concepts of families are commonly derived from folk models. When these categories become objects of attention in discussions and debates they acquire common meanings within a shared way of talking, or discourse (Holstein and Gubrium, 1999). The focus therefore is to examine people's shared language and their intersubjective understandings about family.

Recognizing the social construction of family draws attention to the ways in which people talk about 'the family' as they organize social relationships. People talk about the family as a social unit, and the meanings they give to family affect how they define family membership. For example, James Holstein has studied how family usage varies among community mental health and legal professionals as they make decisions about the cases that come before them (Holstein, 1988). Judgements about the presence or absence of family depend upon such factors as what dimensions of family life are stressed by people occupying different organizational positions. For example, a judge whose main concern is with the living arrangements of someone with mental health problems may draw different conclusions about the presence of family to provide such support than a psychiatrist who is more concerned with the level of psychotherapeutic care. Such local and particular definitions of family are instrumental in shaping how organizations respond to individuals in need of care.

According to Holstein, 'family' is a category that people use to define social bonds, part of a discourse for assigning meaning to relationships. For example, when a social worker says that a client's friends and caregivers are 'like a family' to her, this statement calls upon shared understandings of family ties to convey the caring and supportive nature of the social network. Or, it may be stated that a woman's relatives are 'not really a family' to her at all, indicating the lack of practical support for the tasks of everyday living. Such discourse not only assigns meanings to specific relationships, but it also constructs an image of the family as a source of support and caregiving, and a 'haven in a heartless world' (Gubrium, 1987). In this usage family is defined according to the functions it fulfils, in contrast to defining family on the basis of the structures through which it is enacted.

FAMILY STRUCTURES

Most of our social scientific categorizations of family life are categorizations of family structures. The nuclear family is one type of family structure but it is only one type, as even Murdock recognized. Family structures are sets of relationships in which actors recognize one another, expect certain behaviours from one another, and interact in predictable ways. Interactions may be cooperative, and often are. However, cooperation is not the only predictable form of interaction. Family violence can be as much a part of family structure as love between family members, as we shall see in a later chapter. Families are diverse and show many different characteristics. We will illustrate some of that diversity here by looking at cohabiting couples, single-parent families, extended families, and polygamous families.

Cohabitation

Murdock's definition of the nuclear family was that of a married man and woman and their offspring. One of the reasons why the nuclear family model no longer fits Western societies well is that more and more men and women are now living together without the benefit of marriage. Referred to by social scientists as cohabitation, this pattern of family living has emerged as a challenge to traditional marriage. In many industrial societies, marriage declined from the late 1960s onwards, and this was accompanied by an increase in non-marital cohabitation. Subsequently, the legal difference between marriage and cohabitation was reduced. The decline of legal marriage as a sacred and indissoluble institution seems to be the most significant trend in the evolution of family life in Western societies in recent decades.

Cohabitation has been notably high in Sweden, where it is a normal way of life. It has become more an alternative lifestyle choice there than a prelude to legal marriage, as it may still be elsewhere. In Sweden, the likelihood of subsequent marriage has declined among cohabitors. In other societies, cohabitation is increasingly common among the young, and those who were previously married. In Canada, for example, one half of women and one third of men enter into a cohabiting relationship by age 25 (Wu, 2000). Rates of cohabitation are also high for men and women who have ended their first marriage.

Cohabitation may have become more prevalent, but it can still be a relatively unstable form of family life. For example, in Canada the family life of children born to parents who at some time have cohabitated seems to be particularly unstable (Marcil-Gratton, 1993). Also, consensual unions are significantly more likely to dissolve than formal marriages in Latin America (Desai, 1992). However, a substantial proportion of informal unions are later legalized into formal marriages. This suggests that an element of trial arrangement is often involved in opting for cohabitation. In Canada, only one third of consensual unions survive for three years. The most common reason for terminating a consensual union is marriage of the partners, as more than one half of cohabiting couples eventually get married. For many young Canadians, cohabitation is a short-lived stage in the life course before making the more profound commitment of marriage. More than one third of cohabiting couples marry within three years of moving in together. Apparently there is still some social pressure in Canada to marry, although Canadians now place less value on marriage than they once did. In fact in Canada the social pressure to marry appears to be weakening as a significant minority of cohabitations do not end in marriage.

The shift towards cohabitation in Canada is particularly noticeable in the Province of Quebec. Cohabitation in Quebec is rapidly becoming a replacement of legal marriage, both as the setting for a first union and as a context for the birth of children. It may be a precursor of larger changes to come in the rest of Canada. If a social phenomenon grows more and more common, it means that former negative norms against that phenomenon will be less effective (Trost, 1978). Non-marital cohabitation is clearly losing its marginal character, and it is no longer confined to the role of a trial period for couples who are uncertain about making a long-term commitment.

One subject of interest concerning cohabitation has been its implications for any children of the union. For example, it has been found that in some countries there are higher levels of infant and child mortality among children of mothers in consensual unions than among mothers in legal marriages. Sonalde Desai has hypothesized that this is because partners in less stable unions are more likely to hold on to their personal incomes, and consequently spend less on children than partners in unions based on a greater degree of commitment (Desai, 1992). He supports this hypothesis with research results for northeast Brazil, Colombia and the Dominican Republic. These data show that children whose mothers are in consensual unions are the most likely to be malnourished, and children living with legally married mothers are the least likely to be malnourished. Consistent with the hypothesis of lower investment in children by cohabiting parents, in all three countries children of mothers in consensual unions are significantly more likely to be malnourished than children of mothers in legal unions.

Single-parent families

In addition to cohabitation, another family structure that shows the declining significance of marriage is the single-parent family. Today, more children experience life in a single-parent family than ever before. Single-parent families have received considerable attention in recent years, as their numbers have increased in Western societies. Of course, some single-parent families have always been present. In the past this was usually due to the death of one parent, leaving the other parent behind to care for the children of the union. In Canada, as late as 1960 single-parent families were still formed mainly as a result of mortality (Marcil-Gratton, 1993). The difference between then and now is that today most single-parent families are formed as a result of separation and divorce. It is the increase in the divorce rate that is mainly responsible for the increase in single-parent families.

Growing proportions of Canadian children have experienced life in a single-parent family, and this has been happening earlier in their childhood. However, living in a single-parent family does not necessarily last for a very long time. Children of divorce do not always live for extended periods of time with a single parent, as their parents may remarry. In Canada, the average duration of an episode of living in a single-parent family is approximately four years (Marcil-Gratton, 1993). It follows from this that the number of children who are currently living in a single-parent family underestimates the number of children who have ever lived in a single-parent family. Today, substantial numbers of children have had the experience of living in a single-parent family at some point in their lives.

Single-parent families and extended families

Single-parent families have posed a challenge to policy makers, as the incomes of single parents tend to be lower than those of families containing couples. This has been of notable concern to feminists since most single-parent families are headed by a woman. Particular attention has therefore been paid to poor single-mother families, and in the United States special attention has been paid to poor African-American single-mother families. In recent decades there has been a dramatic increase in the number of families headed by single African-American females. From a situation in which the majority of children lived in families headed by married couples, conditions have changed until today a majority of children live in families headed by single women. Many of these children live below the poverty line. Single parents constitute the majority among the working poor and the underclass. Single-parent-headed households have not only been the fastest growing type of household among African-Americans, but they are also some of the poorest households in America.

Poor single mothers often rely on kin to assist them in the task of child-rearing and to provide practical support in other ways. Steven Ruggles confirms that the high frequency of extended family households among African-Americans has been a means of coping with single parenthood (Ruggles, 1994a). In a study of census microdata for the years between 1880 and 1980, he found that households containing single parents were far more likely to be extended than households without such members. Among African-Americans, and especially among poor African-Americans, extended families provide the context for considerable sharing of resources. They have historically served as a safety net for poor families. This is especially evident in multigenerational households, in which there is a mutual exchange of goods and services. African-Americans, especially those who are poor, are more likely to live in three-generation households than are white families. African-American grandparents, particularly those in poor families, are more likely to be actively involved in rearing their grandchildren than are their white counterparts.

Susan George and Bette Dickerson have studied the role played by grandmothers in poor African-American single-mother families (George and Dickerson, 1995). They report that African-American grandparents in general, and maternal grandmothers in particular, have traditionally provided significant supports for single-parent families. The most common form of support is childcare. The majority of assistance provided to adolescent mothers by individuals comes from their own mothers. Many African-American grandmothers play an important role in the lives of their children and grandchildren, and grandmothers frequently carry out significant tasks in the rearing of grandchildren. This is especially true where the single mothers are adolescents who have not yet completed their education. Among adolescent mothers, the availability of an alternative childcare provider is often critical to enabling them to fulfil their role as mothers as well as staying in school. There are three advantages to this pattern of extended family living. First, having assistance with childcare may allow the young mother to finish school, and consequently increase her chances of employment. Second, the children of adolescent mothers are cared for, at least in part, by more experienced and potentially more capable caregivers than their own mothers. And third, grandmothers may provide, or help to provide, a better home environment than the mother could provide on her own.

However, it would be wrong to assume that all is well in African-American extended families. George and Dickerson suggest that these families have been put under greater strain by the increase in single mothers, and especially by the increase in adolescent single mothers. African-American women are becoming grandmothers at younger ages, which brings them responsibilities that they are not always willing to assume. They may feel that their daughters' expectations of caregiving for grandchildren are inappropriate at their time of life, as these demands have come too early. Women who feel they are too young to be grandmothers are often less ready for this new role, and they are less willing to accept it. They are therefore generally less willing and able to provide additional support to their daughters. This is particularly the case for women who are still working, or who become grandmothers when they are still responsible for raising children of their own. Such women may find the burden of added responsibilities overwhelming, and they may come to resent their daughters' expectations of increased support. What appears to be the case now is that due to the younger ages of these grandmothers they are less likely to take on the traditional role of grandmothering. There is growing concern that the support structure previously provided by grandmothers is beginning to weaken.

Polygyny

Outside Western societies, another form of family life which deviates from the nuclear family model is polygamy. The most common form of polygamy is polygyny, where one man has more than one wife. It may be thought that under the influence of Christian missionaries and Westernization in general, the polygynous family is being replaced by the nuclear family. There is some evidence for this, but it is not always the case, and the polygynous family has certainly not disappeared with modernization. Recent studies have pointed out the persistence, or even the resurgence, of this practice. Contemporary polygyny is found most often in rural areas, but it is certainly not confined to them. In societies where polygyny has been customary, it involves so many people or their close relatives in one way or another that resistance to abolishing it is often strong.

The continued presence of polygyny has been especially challenging to legislators (Pitshandenge, 1994). For example, marriage legislation in Sub-Saharan Africa has moved between modernity and ancestral tradition by either prohibiting or regulating polygyny. Depending on the kind of legislation the state passes, a particular woman may be classified as a wife or a mistress. She and her children may have full rights to inherit her husband's property or no rights at all. Three main legal currents can be identified (Pitshandenge, 1994). One approach has been to mandate monogamy as the exclusive form of marriage with the accompanying prohibition of polygyny. In this system there is an absence of legal protection for polygynous unions. In legal terms, the man and woman have no obligations to care for one another or to support one another in any way. The breakdown of their marriage, which is in effect null, has no legal consequence. A second approach is that of optional marriage. Here, the husband must declare at the time of marriage whether he may take another wife in the future. This system implies a legal recognition of both polygyny and monogamy. Finally, a third approach openly recognizes polygyny, and regulates it with respect to the number of wives a husband may have at one time. This system is found primarily in countries with a strong Muslim tradition.

The place of polygyny in today's world is complex. Thérèse Locoh reports from Togo (a country which has practised optional marriage) that in rural areas the most common marital status among women over age 20 is that of a wife married to a polygynous man with whom she co-resides (Locoh, 1994). In the city of Lomé the situation is different. There, the most common type of marital status is a monogamous union with co-residence of the spouses. With increased schooling in urban areas, the spread of Christianity, the rapid increase in transactions with Western countries, and the diffusion of means of communication, Western notions of monogamy have entered into the culture of Lomé. However, less than half of Lomé residents live in a monogamous union in which the spouses co-reside. Monogamous unions in which the spouses live apart and polygynous unions are also found.

As people have moved from rural areas to urban areas, and their lives have changed in other ways, the institution of polygyny has been adapted to suit changing conditions. The result is a complex array of family forms. Among the urbanized elite, there are those who adopt the nuclear family model, either under the influence of Christianity or out of a desire to be more modern. Outside this group, family living arrangements are more complicated. They may take the form of female-headed households, co-wives living across town from each other, or a man who is theoretically a monogamist but who also has an informal wife. Keeping 'outside wives' who do not reside with their husbands represents elite men's attempt to reconcile Western ideals of modernity (e.g. Christianity, monogamy) with a secret admiration for the African practice of polygyny (Karanja, 1994). Here, public polygyny has been replaced by private polygyny. Outside wives may have regular sexual and financial relations, and even children, with their partners, but their status has no legal recognition. Lomé is a city very much influenced by Christianity and Western styles of life, but its forms of married life are diverse. The diversity of forms of union has elements with roots in both traditional culture and Western culture. Certainly polygyny is still alive and well in the city.

DISCUSSION

In this chapter, we have seen that defining family is a challenging task. Even the most straightforward definition poses insuperable difficulties, as there are so many different types of families. This is especially true when the family is defined, explicitly or implicitly, as the nuclear family. Consensual unions, single-parent families, extended families and polygynous families do not fit the nuclear family model. The term family is an open-ended construct that is created in the ongoing discussions of family members and of professional social scientists. In other words, it is a term whose relevance is defined in social interaction, and its referents vary according to the nature of that interaction.

2 Interaction and meaning in families

Family members construct the reality of their family lives in their ongoing interactions. It is through these interactions that they give meaning to their lives together, and define the expectations that one has of the other. These meanings and expectations vary according to the contexts of interaction, and according to the cultural and ideological assumptions that the actors bring to their interactions. It has been argued that the social construction of family life has taken on an added importance under contemporary conditions, as family relationships are less likely to be governed by traditional norms and well-defined roles. They are also less likely to be affected by the demographic exigencies of uncontrolled childbirth and early death. The overall historical pattern of family behaviour has been marked by a shift from involuntary to voluntary forces controlling family life (Hareven, 1977).

Anthony Giddens has talked about the prevalence today of what he calls the pure relationship. A pure relationship is one which is not maintained by external forces, but its continuation depends upon the interactions of its participants (Giddens, 1991). The individual within the family has to participate in the construction of a private family life rather than having it structured for them (Edgar and Glezer, 1994).

The process that interests us here is one that constructs, maintains and modifies a consistent sense of reality that can be meaningfully experienced by individuals. Marriage is one context in which we can see this process at work (Berger and Kellner, 1964). Every individual requires the ongoing validation of his or her sense of the reality of their world and their definitions of the situations in which they find themselves. This includes, crucially, validation by that handful of people who are their truly significant others. Marriage partners are often among the most significant of these others, but they are not the only significant others. Marriage and marriage-like relationships are often characterized by great intimacy. That is to say these relationships are often physically close, and emotionally and psychologically close. The notion of closeness implies mutual understanding, a shared history of special information, and the communication of positive feelings. The latter is often associated with sexual intimacy. We will first consider the difficulties that some couples have in maintaining their relationships when the normal conditions for intimacy are lacking. It is through such studies that we can reveal the way in which everyday interactions cement relationships. For example, how is the sense of closeness maintained when the partners are not in fact physically close, or can it be maintained in fact?

SEPARATION AND TOGETHERNESS

In the previous chapter we noted that one of the problems with Murdock's definition of the family is that it does not include marriage relationships in which the partners live apart for some of the time. Such relationships challenge the taken-for-granted quality of intimate interaction and they have their own particular dynamics. Since the sense of reality constructed in relationships like marriage depends on the proximity of partners to the relationship, we should expect marriages which separate spouses to render this reality or sense-making function more problematic. This was confirmed in an American study of couples who live apart in order to pursue career goals, which was conducted by Harriet Engel Gross (1980). These couples had a strong emotional investment in their relationship, and they wanted to preserve the quality of their relationship despite the threats to it posed by their current lifestyle. They accepted a view of marriage as intimate and emotionally close, but they found it hard to maintain this in practice.

Gross found that separated marriage partners frequently missed the little conversations about the day's doings that co-resident couples take for granted. Even couples who communicated regularly by telephone reported missing the ability to talk to each other on a casual basis. They regretted not being able to engage in discussions about everyday things through which many couples construct the meaning of their relationship. What these couples call attention to is not a special interest in the details of everyday life, but rather that such exchanges between spouses deepen their intimacy and their sense of involvement with one another.

Couples who spent some time apart often found it difficult to re-establish their relationship when they eventually got together. They talked about their initial contact when they came together again as being 'strange' or 'weird', and they reported not knowing what to talk about at first. Couples who got together for a short time only, say just a weekend, found this especially difficult. By the time the partners were comfortable with one another again, it was time to get ready to separate. This was less of a problem for couples who were apart during the week, but who got together on a regular basis at the weekends. For these couples their time together fitted into the normal routine of time for leisure and family at the weekends. They found it easier to re-establish the marital conversation than couples who got together less frequently or on an irregular basis. Re-establishing contact was also harder for couples in which one or both partners had established a new residence. This might be done for reasons of cost, since maintaining two residences is expensive, by, for example, taking on a cheaper apartment. The one who visited her or his partner in their new residence often reported feeling ill-at-ease and out of place. This shows the importance of having a common residence, a shared space, to maintaining the meaning of marriage. Family, in fact, is often identified with the home.

HOME AND FAMILY

The concept of home as we know it in Western societies has not always existed, and the close identification of family with home is a relatively recent phenomenon (Hareven, 1991). In Europe and America it came into existence between the end of the eighteenth century and the middle of the nineteenth century, during a period of considerable change in family life. The development of the concept of home was closely related to the development of the family as a private, emotional unit. By the middle of the nineteenth century, the home had emerged as a physical and symbolic space different from other spaces. It was a place for private retreat and the cultivation of nuclear family relationships. In the pre-industrial household, many activities including work activities were carried out in the domestic dwelling, and households often contained individuals who were not related by blood or marriage but who contributed to carrying out everyday tasks. There was little privacy, and no attempt to separate off nuclear family members from other members of the household. The development of the concept of the home as a private retreat for the nuclear family was associated with the separation of work from family activities, and the separation of nuclear family members from outsiders. Factories and businesses took over the production functions of the household, schools took over the family's former educational functions, and asylums and correctional institutions took over the family's functions of welfare and social control. Family members were no longer connected through their work, and family time became restricted primarily to the home. The house was redefined as the family's private retreat, as a specialized site for the family's consumption, child-rearing and private life. A new identification of home and nuclear family emerged.

From the early nineteenth century on, 'home' began to assume an enormous symbolic meaning among the urban middle class. The symbolically constructed home that had emerged by mid-century had a meaning different from other spaces. It was there that people experienced togetherness and happiness. It became the special responsibility of women to maintain the home as a sanctuary for family life. Wives became the priestesses of the cult of domesticity, arranging the family home so as to be a comfortable and relaxing environment for their husbands when they returned home from work. Women, home and family stood against the uncaring world of industrial work. In this new family system it became inappropriate for middle-class women to work outside the home. Women now had to focus on the home and the family, and housework and cooking became extremely significant for the maintenance of the perfect home. The emergence of the home as the family's private retreat was closely linked to the new definition of women as confined to the private sphere, which stressed the role of the wife as homemaker and mother.

The ideal of a tranquil home life not only required redefining the role of women, but it also required the spatial relocation of the household. The ideal middle-class home came to be identified with life in the suburbs, away from the pressures and distractions of city life. From the 1870s on, many Americans moved into the suburbs to fulfil their dream of a tranquil home life removed from the city (Hareven, 1991). This ideal has persisted into the twenty-first century, and it cuts across all classes. However, its context is different today.

By the latter part of the twentieth century, the identification of family and home had become part of a traditional family ideology. For example, in a household survey in three towns in England conducted in the mid-1980s it was found that people's principal image of their homes was family, children, love and affection (Saunders, 1989). For some people, the home literally means a family life. This image was shared equally by men and women. According to Saunders, men and women both still share a sense of home as a haven. For both men and women, the home is experienced in a positive way as a place where they can relax, be themselves, establish their own rules of conduct, and feel secure in the midst of their family. Men and women in England diverge markedly in the typical domestic tasks that they perform, but these differences do not seem to generate any significant variation in their attachment to the home as a private haven.

Lyn Richards has examined this traditional family ideology, and its contradictions, in a suburb of Melbourne, Australia (Richards, 1989). There, the traditional family ideology is a still a gendered ideology. Women are equated with the private sphere and men with the public sphere. In this ideology, home, and women's place within it, are central features of family life, in which the home epitomizes the private world of domesticity.

In Australia, ideas of a congenial home life tend to be equated with the ideal of home ownership. As one woman said, 'We want to be a family, and a good foundation is owning your own home.' For many couples in the suburb of Green Views, owning one's own home is seen as a necessary part of becoming an independent married couple and a necessary condition for having children. It is seen as good for the children, a secure and comfortable place in which they can grow up.

Home ownership is seen as the proper path to guaranteeing financial security for the family, as well as providing a home base in which the members are free to do as they please. In this ideology of home and family, notions of privacy and having a haven from the outside world are linked to ideas about independence, control, security, being settled down and permanence. Home ownership is idealized in part because it is something that a couple build up together, it is part of their togetherness. Home ownership is seen as a unifying principle in married life. It is tangible proof of a couple's success in creating a family. Home ownership also provides an incentive to stay at home, to maintain and fix up the property. It thus centres the individual's life in home and family. Or does it?

There is a contradiction in the ideology of home and family in places like Green Views. Women, whose activities are seen as central to providing a satisfactory home life, must usually work outside the home in order to help pay the mortgage. In today's version of family life, women tend to be employed outside the home in order to improve the family's standard of living and maintain a desirable family lifestyle. In Green Views, family values retain major elements of traditional family ideology. The family and home are women's priorities, and a woman's place is in the home. Yet women cannot be home if the home ownership they aspire to is to be realized. The home which provides a central basis for motivating everyday activities is therefore usually empty during the day. In a suburb sold as a 'family community' it is common to find that nobody is home.

RITUALIZATION OF FAMILY LIFE

Home and family are seen by most people in modern societies as standing in opposition to the meanings of employment in the market economy. Opposition between the meanings of family and work has been a general problem since the emergence of an unfettered market economy in capitalist society. Work relations in capitalism are dominated by an ethic of individual competitiveness, which guarantees success only to those who disregard personal feelings in order to engage in the struggle for economic resources. Family relations are based mainly on feelings of love and commitment, in which the continuity of relationships is guaranteed by the strength of emotional bonds. But how to express the strength of these bonds in the face of a dominant market economy is a practical problem.

John Gillis has explained that one way of doing this has been through the ritualization of family ties (Gillis, 1989). He has traced the emergence of such rituals as Christmas, the family vacation and the white wedding in Victorian Britain to the need felt by the middle class to differentiate their family life from their work life. He argues that Victorian middle-class family life became ritualized in the middle of the nineteenth century because this was one of the ways in which the bourgeoisie could resolve the problems of meaning arising from the capitalist industrial society that they had themselves created. The widespread practice and staying power of these rituals, which have now become traditions, suggests that today these problems affect almost everyone in modern society. Since family relations are not grounded in the modern system of production, family members have adjusted to capitalist society by developing supportive practices such as family-oriented Christmas rituals. Family life in capitalist societies takes the form of a private world that is separated from the public world of industrial production and economic exchange (Berger, Berger and Kellner, 1973; Laslett, 1973; Zaretsky, 1976). Ritual transactions, such as Christmas dinners and exchanges of Christmas presents, provide the basis for interaction and emotional identification that was once provided by cooperative labour.

Historically, the economy was based on the household. In addition to serving as the family's place of residence and the focus for the family's various domestic activities, the household was the site of production. Commitment to individual economic success and family ties therefore posed no problem. As late as the eighteenth and early nineteenth centuries, when family meant all the members of the household economy, economic relations were family relations. Also, the working wife's role was not yet at odds with that of motherhood, and a father's business did not remove him from daily contact with his children. As long as the household remained the unit of production as well as consumption, work time and family time were quite undifferentiated. Up to the 1840s, family time was the same as any other time, family space the same as any other space, without any special meaning or symbolization. Communities and religious groups had their special days and sacred places, but not families. Birthdays, for example, were private moments for the individual to review his or her spiritual accounts, not the family occasions they were later to become.

Around the middle of the nineteenth century, the relationships between household, home and family changed. The middle-class house became separated from the outside world both symbolically and physically, thus transforming the house into a home. The home became a space clearly separated from work and its meanings, and it was the site for family, which now became separated from workers such as servants. Following the removal of the workplace from the household as a result of urbanization and industrialization, the household was recast as the family's private retreat and home emerged as a new concept. A concept of the home as the family's haven from the pressures of the outside world emerged (Hareven, 1991). A firm distinction between work time and family time mirrored the split between home and the outside world. Family time was neither work nor leisure but something special. Rituals were introduced to define this new symbolic world. For example, father's departure for work, and his return home from work, were given new symbolic significance. Homecoming restored to the man those family feelings and connections that he was forced to ignore in the impersonal world of the market economy. The home and the rituals of homecoming were inventions of a modern era facing new problems of meaning. These problems were created by a capitalist economy that separated family and production, and which made it necessary for men to deny family feelings in their work.

Daily homecoming rituals were reinforced by weekly and annual occasions. For example, Sunday became the most important family day of the week, epitomized by the big family dinner. Christmas also became ritualized as a family occasion. The Christmas tree, gift giving, and Santa Claus were introduced as new rituals that celebrated family life. In the past, children's involvement with Christmas had been minimal. Now they, and their relations with their parents, were placed at the centre of the new Christmas. Previously, Christmas had been a communal occasion, and hospitality and gifts had flowed from the rich to the poor. But the new family Christmas turned inward. Gift exchange was limited mainly to family members, and children rather than the poor were the main beneficiaries. Through Christmas rituals men gained symbolic access to the world of childhood, and thus to the feelings and connections that were missing in their working lives. By playing the role of Santa, fathers could exchange their everyday role as workers for that of altruistic gift givers. In this way fathers, whose work separated them from the home, could re-establish their connections with their children and other family members.

GIFT GIVING

In modern society, one of the characteristics of family relations is that they are distinguished by the giving and receiving of gifts. Gift giving on ritual occasions such as Christmas reaffirms the continued importance of family ties. It is a means by which individuals communicate the meanings of the relationships that they have with their significant others. Giving something tangible shows the love and appreciation that one person has for another, and it therefore contributes to the reproduction of a private world of family relationships.

Love can be shown in a variety of ways. In a study of gift giving in Winnipeg, Canada, David Cheal found that there were five different ways in which love could be communicated (Cheal, 1987). They are: the labour value of a gift, the symbolic significance of a gift, the number of gifts, the utility of a gift, and the financial value of a gift. First, the labour value of a gift refers to the time and effort that the giver put into selecting it. According to this view, giving a gift object is worth more than giving money because in the former case the giver took the time to select an appropriate object. Sacrificing one's time is even more marked in gifts that are hand-made, which have a special value. Second, the symbolic significance of a gift is the value that a gift has simply by virtue of being marked as a gift. For example, gift objects are usually gift-wrapped or marked in other ways, such as having ribbons tied round them. Third, people may signify the special importance of their significant others by giving a number of gifts. This can be done by giving gifts on a number of occasions throughout the year, or by giving multiple gifts on one occasion. Fourth, in order to be successful communication devices, gifts must be sufficiently interesting that they attract attention. The only certain way of doing this is to give a gift that is useful to the recipient so that it is in fact used in everyday life. And fifth, there is the financial value of the gift. This is an especially important consideration where monetary gifts are concerned. For example, people do not always know what to give to others, because they do not know what they need, and giving money can be a solution to this problem.

Gifts are one way of defining a private world of love and ritual which is different from, and in contrast to, the impersonal capitalist economy. Yet gift giving in modern society is affected by that economy. This is most obvious in the case of monetary gifts, whose value lies entirely in the capacity to purchase things in the marketplace. However, it also exists in the case of gifts of things where those gifts consist, as most do, of things that are purchased. There is a problem here. In advanced capitalist societies, consumption by individuals of things that they do not produce is a massive activity. There is a danger here that purchased gifts will lose their significance in the face of all the things that individuals purchase for themselves. Gift giving separates a world of love and ritual from the capitalist economy, but in the end the two systems of meaning cannot be entirely separated because they are interconnected.

DISCUSSION

In this chapter we have looked at the modern meanings of family life and how they are sustained by interactions of certain kinds. We have also seen how historical changes in the capitalist economy created problems in sustaining the meaning of family life, leading to a new definition of home and the ritualization of family interaction. One of the implications of the changed definition of family life is that the position of women in family life also changed, especially in the middle classes. In the second half of the nineteenth century, middle-class women were excluded from the sphere of paid employment and given a new role as homemakers. It was their responsibility to create a world of love and ritual to which their husbands could retreat from their workaday lives. A profound division was thus introduced between the roles of wives and husbands, reminding us that family life is as much about creating divisions as it is about creating unity.

3 Social divisions

Social divisions can occur between families or within families. The former include divisions of race and class between families with different characteristics, the latter include divisions of age and sex between people occupying different roles within families. In this chapter, both types of division are discussed, beginning with divisions within families. Gender, the social construction of sex differences, has received special attention (Ferree, 1990). That is mainly due to a renewed interest in the connection between women and family life. Part of the reason for this is that women's lives have been changing, and with it their position in family life. The other part of the reason for a renewed interest in the connection between women and family life is the impact of feminism. From this perspective, gender is identified as a basic structural feature of families (Glenn, 1987). Feminist analyses share the view that gendered inequalities and power relations are inherent features of family structure.

GENDER AND FAMILY

Feminists have been critical of what they see as women's subordination in family life under the influence of patriarchy, as well as the barriers that traditional family roles have posed to women's economic and social advancement. They have therefore worked actively to encourage women to change their family lives. As a result, they have focused on the differences between women's and men's experiences and interests within families. Instead of looking at the family as a unit, they have tended to see families as sites of struggle and conflict. Evelyn Nakano Glenn, for example, has remarked that when demographers talk about 'family decisions' to limit family size they ignore the long history of struggle between men and women over reproduction (Glenn, 1987). Sexual behaviour is also something that can provoke conflicts between women and men. Annie George has observed in a study of sexual relations in a low-income area of Mumbai, India that wives and husbands had significantly different perspectives on sexual pleasure, sexual coercion, and beliefs about male and female sexuality (George, 1998). Women were commonly asked to have sex against their wishes, while many men felt they had a right to sex in marriage. These differences resulted in ongoing negotiations about having or avoiding sex. She concludes that the difference in power between husbands and wives is significant in shaping the outcome of sexual negotiations. Among the factors that constrain women's ability to control their sexual lives is their economic dependency on men.

Heidi Hartmann has argued that family is a location where people with different activities and interests come into conflict with one another (Hartmann, 1981). One of the things they come into conflict over, she thinks, is housework. Women do more housework than men. The rather small and selective contribution of the husband to housework can create resentment in the wife, and lead to conflict over who does what. One of the reasons why women's position in these conflicts has been weaker than that of men has been their economic dependency upon the wages of their husbands. That is because dependent wives have less power, whereas wives play a greater part in their family's decision-making if they are in paid, particularly full-time, employment. Insofar as wives need the significantly higher economic resources of their husbands, part of the cost to be paid is their willingness to submit to the power of their husbands. Yet changes have been occurring here. Are wives still dependent on their husbands, and what trends can be observed?

WIVES' ECONOMIC DEPENDENCY AND GENDER INEQUALITY

Married women's economic dependence is inextricably linked to their place in a gender division of labour. It has reflected mainly a division between men and women in their work for pay. Men work more hours of paid employment outside the home, and women perform more domestic responsibilities inside the home. On average, wives in Western societies contribute less financially to family life than their husbands, because they are less likely to work outside the home, they work fewer hours when they are employed, and their earnings are lower. Insofar as there is a redistribution of income from husbands to wives, wives are dependent upon the wages of their husbands (Sorensen, 1994). The extent of the redistribution is a measure of their economic dependency.

Feminist theorists concerned with patterns of gender inequality have identified married women's economic dependency as one of the central mechanisms by which women's subordinate position in family life is maintained. That is because power differentials between husbands and wives are directly related to differences in contributions to family income. Annemette Sorensen and Sara McLanahan believe that economic dependency is a problem for married women (Sorensen and McLanahan, 1987). For one thing, it becomes the basis for individual women making decisions that limit their position in the labour market, and it has helped to justify paying lower wages to women.

Wives' economic dependency is also a disadvantage to them should they lose their husbands through death or divorce, as their standard of living will fall (Sorensen, 1994). Divorced mothers in particular are far more likely to receive a lower income than are divorced fathers (Ward, Dale and Joshi, 1996). The gains that women may make from their marital dependence on men come at the risk of increased economic vulnerability. Insofar as they are dependent, wives are exposed to greater risks of poverty and economic insecurity than are husbands. Few dependent women can sell their domestic services in the marketplace and expect to receive an income equivalent to that which they received from their spouse. Annemette Sorensen has concluded from a study of women's economic risk in the United States, Germany and Sweden that married mothers' economic dependence means that they will face enormous changes in economic position if they have to rely solely on their current earnings after divorce (Sorensen, 1994). In contrast, the economic implications for married fathers are much less. Even if the father continues to live with the children (which is usually not the case) his own earnings will guarantee almost no change in economic position. This gender division in the economic implications of divorce was found to be greatest in Germany, because married mothers' economic dependency is highest in that country by comparison with Sweden and the United States.

Sorensen and McLanahan have studied wives' economic dependency in the United States, and they find that it has decreased since 1940. Traditionally, almost all women stopped working as soon as they got married. In 1940, the vast majority of married women were completely dependent upon their spouses for economic support, and the average level of dependency was correspondingly very high. Today, American wives who are completely dependent constitute a distinct minority, and the average level of dependency is much lower than it was earlier. The rise in women's labour-force participation has increased their incomes, and it has reduced their dependency upon their husbands. In particular, there has been a dramatic decline in the number of women who contribute nothing to family income. Nevertheless, these very significant changes mainly reflect a change from complete dependence to some dependence.

Significant numbers of wives continue to be economically dependent upon their husbands, more so among white women than among non-white women.

Michel Van Berkel and Nan Dirk De Graaf have replicated Sorensen and McLanahan's analysis in a study of married women's economic dependency in the Netherlands (Van Berkel and De Graaf, 1998). They find that Dutch wives' economic dependency too is decreasing. In 1979, more than 70 per cent of married women were completely dependent economically. By 1991 this had decreased to less than half of wives making no contribution to the couple's family income. Nevertheless, significant numbers of Dutch wives remain completely or largely economically dependent, and their number is greater than in the United States. The wife relies on an income transfer from her husband for more than 50 per cent of her standard of living in two out of three couples. In Dutch society, a wife's economic dependence on her husband is still taken for granted, especially if she has children.

In a similar study in Britain, Clare Ward, Angela Dale and Heather Joshi observe that women's economic dependency is still strongly influenced by the primacy given to domestic and childcare work (Ward, Dale and Joshi, 1996). Some women reduce their paid work upon marriage, and more reduce their hours of work when they are responsible for children. The norm for employed fathers in Britain is to have full-time employment, whereas most employed mothers have part-time jobs, with a substantial proportion working fewer than 16 hours a week (Brannen and Moss, 1998). Not surprisingly, economic dependency is still the norm for a majority of wives in Britain, and the association between economic dependency and having children is marked. Childless women are far more likely to contribute equally to, or more than, their partners compared with women with children. In particular, childless women working full-time are the only ones for whom the majority are not dependent on their partners.

The difference between women with children and women without children reminds us that not all women are the same. There are divisions between women according to their social experiences and social locations. For example, Sorensen and McLanahan have found that women's economic dependency in the United States varies by race. Reflecting racial divisions between families, non-white women are consistently less dependent economically than white women, and the difference between them appears to have increased over time. This is just one way in which African-American families differ from white families.

RACE AND FAMILY TIES

Family ties differ by race, and one of the differences is the tendency to form extended family households. In the United States, for example, living in extended family households is more common among racial and ethnic minorities than it is among Whites. Natalia Sarkisian, Mariana Gerena and Naomi Gerstel have examined this and other differences between Mexicans, Puerto Ricans and Whites living in the United States (Sarkisian, Gerena and Gerstel, 2006). They found that both groups of Latinos/as are significantly more likely to co-reside with kin and to live within two miles of their relatives. Turning to kin support, both Mexicans and Puerto Ricans were found to be less likely than Whites to give substantial financial assistance, though Mexicans, but not Puerto Ricans, are more likely than Whites to provide instrumental help.

One of the issues in the study of racial divisions in family practices has been whether the most potent explanations are for structural variables as opposed to cultural variables. In other words, are most of the differences between the races to be explained by different distributions of social positions or are they to be explained by different ideas about family life? The answer to this question is that in general the greatest influence seems to be from structural factors. One structural factor is position in a structure of family roles. This factor was found by Sarkisian *et al.* to be relevant in the provision of instrumental help. People who have more children, and who do not have a partner to help them, are in greater need of practical assistance from kin and are more likely to engage in the exchange of instrumental support. Mexicans were found to be in a less favourable position than Whites in both respects and therefore they exchanged more instrumental help. In the statistical analysis by Sarkisian *et al.*, higher fertility and higher rates of single parenthood among Mexicans as compared with Whites explained the ethnic difference in instrumental help.

Another structural factor is social class position. As we might expect, socioeconomic position has a great influence on the provision of financial support. People with higher incomes, wealth, education and employment are more likely to give financial help than those with a lower socioeconomic position, whereas receipt of public assistance is associated with a lesser likelihood of giving significant money gifts. Whites tend to have higher socioeconomic positions than Latinos/as, and they are therefore more likely to be financial benefactors. Similarly, socioeconomic variables account for most of the variation in whether or not people live within two miles of their relatives. More education and higher income are associated with a lower likelihood of living near kin, presumably because people with more education and higher incomes are more likely to be occupationally and geographically mobile. Because Whites have higher socioeconomic positions on average than Latinos/as, they are less likely to reside close to kin.

Sarkisian *et al.* found that where differences in co-residence were concerned, the most important factors were again structural variables. To be specific, differences in socioeconomic position had a greater effect on the tendency to form extended family households than differences in ideas about family life. Having a low income is often associated with a higher likelihood of co-residing, and because Latinos/as had lower incomes than Whites they were more likely to co-reside with their kin. However, cultural differences also had an effect on living arrangements, albeit a minor one. Differences in preferences for extended family supports, and differences in attitudes towards traditional gender roles, were both found to be related to family living arrangements. Preference for extended family living is clearly a complex phenomenon.

We can see the complexity of family living arrangements in the fact that extended family households are not always formed for the same reasons. Sometimes extended family households are formed when an unmarried teenage daughter and her child remain in her parents' household or when an adult child and her children return to the parental household to live. This type of household is said to be formed through downward extension, as the reason for forming the extended family household is to provide financial assistance and/or childcare for the younger generations. In contrast, other intergenerational extended family households are formed through upward extension. Here, the extended family household is formed in order to provide care and support for aged parents, when they are either too ill or too frail to look after themselves or when they become widowed. According to Maximiliane Szinovacz, there are variations between racial and ethnic groups in America in the tendency to form intergenerational extended family households for one or other of these reasons (Szinovacz, 1996).

Szinovacz found from a nationally representative survey of US households that upward extension constitutes the more common form of household extension among Whites, but among African-Americans downward extension is the more common form of household extension. Downward extension is related to family structure. Respondents who did not grow up with both parents are significantly more likely to have lived with grandparents than those who did. Downward extension seems to occur mainly as a response to family crises, and it is most likely to be found among families in which grandchildren either do not grow up in nuclear families or they experience disruptions in their nuclear families.

Divorce and teenage parenthood lead to an increased parenting role by grandparents and to the formation of households containing both grandparents and grandchildren.

In statistical analyses, controlling for family structure reduces but does not eliminate the effect of being African-American upon downward extension. This suggests that part of the difference between the races in the tendency to form households that offer support to the younger generations is due to differences in family structure. However, that is not the entire story. There also appear to be cultural differences between the races in the preference for downward extension. African-American grandparents assume a more influential role in the lives of their grand-children, and they are more likely to take grandchildren into their households than white grandparents.

African-American families

The most striking difference between African-American families and white families is that African-Americans are far more likely than Whites to become single parents and to reside in extended families. Various theories have been expounded for these differences, including the influence of traditional African cultures, the experience of slavery, and the effects of living in poverty. Recent research suggests that the African-American family pattern has a long history, but that it has also been influenced by recent social and economic changes.

Steven Ruggles has examined African-American family structure using census microdata for the century from 1880 to 1980 (Ruggles, 1994a). His data show that African-Americans have been consistently more likely to live in single-parent families than Whites throughout this period. Among Whites, the numbers living in single-parent families fell between 1940 and 1960, and then rose again from 1960 to 1980 to a level comparable to the earlier historical period. Among African-Americans, the numbers living in single-parent families were relatively stable over the period from 1880 to 1960 but then increased dramatic-ally between 1960 and 1980 to a level almost three times that of Whites. Concerning extended family living, this form of household has declined among both African-Americans and Whites, particularly since 1940 among Whites and since 1960 among African-Americans. How-ever, African-Americans remained two-and-a-half times more likely than Whites to be living in extended families at the end of the period.

These data support the argument that the distinctive features of African-American families have deep historical roots, but they also indicate the importance of recent changes. Although the origins of the characteristic patterns of African-American families can be traced back to the nineteenth century, race differences have become more pronounced over the course of the twentieth century, especially in later decades. Changes that can be invoked to explain the growing differential between African-American family structure and white family structure include the declining economic position of African-American men, and the increased impact of growing up in poverty. Income level makes a difference to family life, including family structure.

INCOME POVERTY

Family income is a major determinant of lifestyle and life chances. For example, a number of studies find powerful effects of income upon health as well as psychological and social development (Duncan, 1996; Brooks-Gunn and Duncan, 1997; Duncan *et al.*, 1998). Average income level is found to have a strong association with mortality. Individuals living in families with low income have a probability of death that is three times higher than individuals living in high-income families. Also, children's physical and psychological development is affected by their family's income level. Children in persistently poor families have a higher prevalence of stunting and wasting, lower IQs and more behaviour problems than children who have not lived in persistent poverty. Particularly high correlations seem to be found between family income and children's ability as well as their reading and maths achievement. In the case of the cognitive development of children, income matters because it is connected with a richer learning environment. A number of studies have found that a child's home environment accounts for a substantial portion of the effects of family income on cognitive outcomes in children. Early childhood appears to be the stage in which family economic conditions matter the most.

Studies of children's early physical and cognitive development suggest that family income in the first five years of life is highly correlated with developmental outcomes in early and middle childhood. And similarly, family income is found to be linked to developmental outcomes in adolescence and early adulthood. This includes the probability of completed schooling and early-adult success in the labour market, as well as the probability of having children out of wedlock. Lower parental income is associated with a higher probability that teenage girls will experience a non-marital birth. The rate of out-of-wedlock births among poor teens is almost three times as high as the rate among those from non-poor families. These results suggest that family income is a powerful determinant of health and development, and they are independent of family characteristics associated with low income. Children who live in extreme poverty, or who live below the poverty line for a number of years, appear to suffer the worst outcomes. Among the families with children who are most likely to be poor are single-parent families.

FAMILY CHARACTERISTICS AND FAMILY INCOME

Family income varies greatly by family structure. Chris Tilly and Randy Albelda find that in the United States disparities between family types account for a substantial portion of total family earnings inequality (Tilly and Albelda, 1994). Family head characteristics, such as education and race, account for only part of the differences among family types. The largest factor in earnings inequality among family types is the total number of hours spent in the labour force. Families such as dual-income couples spend a large number of hours in the labour force while families headed by single parents spend fewer hours in the labour force.

Some types of families do very well economically, whereas others fare very poorly. For example, single-mother headed families have very low earnings on average, while young childless couples have very high earnings. A central concern has been the plight of single mothers, whose choices are particularly constrained by their economic position. Single-mother families have only one working-age adult, and they are more likely to contain young children who have the biggest negative impact on labour force participation. Single mothers suffer the greatest income disadvantage, and their average income adjusted for family needs is even below that of the elderly (Tilly and Albelda, 1994). This disadvantage is relatively independent of the business cycle.

Employment is not distributed evenly across family characteristics. In a study in Britain, Brannen and Moss report that mothers were more likely to be employed if they were in a couple household living with an employed partner, and had older children or fewer children (Brannen and Moss, 1998). In contrast, mothers were less likely to be employed if they were single parents, and had younger children or three or more children. Brannen and Moss report that these differences in employment were accentuated over the decade between 1984 and 1994. For example, employment increased strongly among mothers with partners, from 50 per cent to 64 per cent. By comparison, it retreated slightly among single mothers, from 41 per cent to 39 per cent. The economic division between children growing up in different types of families appears to have been increasing in Britain.

Growing earnings inequality between families in Britain is partly a result of changes in the number of earners per household. But it is not entirely due to that. It is also a result of changing differences in earning power due to disparities in educational qualifications. This points to the continued impact of class position on family life.

DISCUSSION

Recent analyses of social divisions and families have tended to focus upon gender. That is for two reasons. First, gender divisions continue to exist within families. We have seen this here in the fact that significant numbers of wives continue to be economically dependent upon their husbands, with all the implications that entails for inequalities in power in family life. Second, gender is a relevant factor in differences between types of families, and also in racial divisions. The biggest single issue here consists of the prevalence of, and consequences of, single-parent families, most of which are headed by women. Families headed by single mothers do less well financially than couple families, and, as we have seen, differences in income have effects on health and the development of children. Inequalities between women in different types of families therefore deserve attention, especially when they appear to have been changing.

Women's lives have been changing in recent decades, in some cases dramatically. We have seen this here in the effect of women's greater employment for wages upon their reduced levels of economic dependency, especially in the United States. We have also seen it in the consequences of increased employment among married mothers for greater inequalities between them and single mothers in Britain. Social change is one of the principal characteristics of modern families.

4 Social change

Families are changing everywhere, and in this chapter we shall consider some of the changes that have been happening in different parts of the world. If there is one master trend, it is that of individualization. Individuals have become differentiated from families and have acquired greater autonomy. As they have gained autonomy, they have made personal decisions about their family relationships. These decisions, about such things as whether to marry or cohabit, or indeed whether to live alone, or whether to divorce or stay married, have implications for family structure. For example, a study of family change in France, Germany, Quebec and the USA between 1960 and 1990 found a substantial increase in the number of one-person households as a proportion of all households, especially in Quebec (Bahr *et al.*, 1994). In Western societies, marriage rates have fallen, people get married for the first time at older ages, divorce and cohabitation have risen, people have fewer children and there has been a marked increase in the proportion of people living by themselves or living alone with dependent children. As these changes have occurred, the proportion of people living in the traditional nuclear family has declined.

Outside Western societies, some of the strongest effects of individualism are felt in decisions about courtship and marriage. Traditionally, parents often had considerable influence over their children's choice of marriage partners, if marriages were not arranged outright by the parents. But with urbanization, industrialization and modernization, adult children have acquired greater independence and greater control over the timing of marriage and the choice of partner. For example, in recent decades there has been a transformation from arranged marriages to free-choice marriages in urban China (Xu, 1998). In Thailand, many young women migrate to Bangkok in search of better opportunities for themselves, as well as to earn money to send home to their parents who remain in the rural areas. Living away from their parents, and having an independent wage, has given them greater personal control over their lives. Traditionally, courtship rituals enabled young women's families to encourage or discourage particular romantic attachments, and formal arrangements for marriage were in the hands of parents and elders. But in the city, young, migrant women are able to engage in dating away from the supervision of their parents, and sometimes this leads to marriage with partners who have not been approved by their parents (Mills, 1998). Migrants and their rural families all acknowledge that urban opportunities for following contemporary ideals of romance have given young people greater influence over courtship decisions than was true in the past. Sometimes this means that parents must negotiate a formal engagement after a couple have already made their choice and taken the first steps towards marriage, and at other times it means accepting the fait accompli of a marriage that has already taken place in the city. If parents do attempt to arrange marriages for their migrant children, the children may deliberately stay in the city in order to avoid an unwanted match. Parents complain that they have lost influence over their children's marital decisions, and they say that now they simply have to go along with the children's wishes. Another complaint is that their daughters do not send enough money home, as the young women seek to retain more of their wages to establish a life for themselves in the city. Young women living in Bangkok are very attracted by the image of the beautiful, independent, modern young woman and the related standards of consumption portrayed in the mass media. Experimenting with clothing and cosmetics, and spending money on leisure activities, become part of a new way of life that is distinctly different from parental values. These new criteria of the good life come to rival the traditional values of family-centred living. The commodification of women that permeates Bangkok life contrasts sharply with household-based standards of feminine modesty.

Although individualism has increased, this may not mean that family life has become any less important. The decline in nuclear family households in the West, with the increase in the proportion of people living alone, or alone with dependent children, and changing marriage practices in developing countries, have led some observers to claim that individualism has replaced family life as the focus of people's concerns. For some this has been seen as a good thing, for others it has been seen as a bad thing presaging the decline of the family. But it is not necessarily the case that family life has eroded. For example, in Thailand most young, migrant women living in Bangkok retain close ties with family members living in the countryside, visiting at least once a year or more, and almost all of them plan to return home. Most women assert their intention to marry some day, although they are ambivalent about when and how to do so. In the West, another example of the persisting importance of family is that the increase in one-person households in Quebec between 1961 and 1986 was due more to a retreat from living in non-family households containing multiple persons, than it was to a decline in living in family households (Bahr *et al.*, 1994). In Europe, the most common living arrangement is still to live in a family, as more than four out of five people reside in a family household (Solsona, 1998). Further, the growing instability of marriage with increasing divorce does not necessarily mean that there is a crisis in family life. Rather, it may be the result of the increasing expectations that individuals have with regard to the quality of family relationships. Much is expected of marriage today. Hence, it does not seem appropriate to talk about 'the end of the family'. Instead, we should talk about a new diversity of family forms.

Outside the household, frequency of contact between parents and non-co-resident children has changed very little in France, Germany and the USA in recent years, as computed from adult children's reports, and there is continuity in the patterns of helping behaviour between parents and their adult children (Bahr *et al.*, 1994). Jacqueline Scott has concluded from survey research in Britain that family issues and events continue to be at the forefront of attention for most people (Scott, 1997). Individuals often maintain emotional and material links with family members, whether or not they live with them. Kinship ties continue to be important, and one of the distinguishing features of kin relationships is that they are relatively durable while friendship and work relationships are often temporary because of occupational and geographic mobility. The strength of kinship ties does not seem to have changed much in Western societies in recent years. Intergenerational relations, especially between parents and their adult children, continue to be among the most important social relationships outside the nuclear family, and they tend to be maintained throughout the lives of the parents. But is that also the case elsewhere? How kinship ties are maintained under changing conditions is often most evident today in the developing world.

CHANGING KINSHIP TIES

Modernization theory has hypothesized that industrialization, urbanization, and the growth of modern social institutions such as the welfare state have all led to the declining importance of kinship ties. Greater geographic mobility pulls extended families apart, as frequency of interaction decreases dramatically with greater physical separation. Also, the expansion of other spheres of interest means that other systems of meaning rival family meanings. Achievement is emphasized rather than ascription, and universalistic values are stressed rather than particularistic values. Also, to the extent that the welfare state is developed, people look to the state for much of the protection and economic security that was once provided by extended kin. On the other hand, kinship ties may actually be strengthened by industrialization, modernization and urbanization. For example, among the possible effects of migration are a concentration and intensification of kinship ties. Living in a city, with its diversity of occupations, may actually reduce people's need to migrate in search of employment, and thereby increase their opportunity to live near kin. Also, greater longevity that is associated with modernization means that there are more elderly parents and other relatives available for interaction. The possibility for intergenerational kinship ties therefore expands with modernization.

In recent decades, social change has been particularly rapid in many places in the developing world. This is most notably the case in Asia, in countries such as Korea and Taiwan which have experienced unprecedented social change since the 1960s. If kinship ties have been weakening anywhere, it should be most evident there. One dimension of kinship ties is co-residence. In both Korea and Taiwan the number of people co-residing with their parents has declined (Marsh and Hsu, 1995; Lee, 1999). This is partly due to the effects of urbanization. Young people migrate from the rural areas to the cities, leaving their parents behind. This does not indicate a breaking of family ties, however, as the parents support the migration in order to enhance the economic prosperity of the family. Also, while living in separate residences, the adult children tend to retain strong bonds with their parents and other relatives. In modern Korea, although the traditional kin-consciousness has been weakened, many urban residents expect to live near their close kin (Lee, 1999). Close relatives are the primary network for emotional support, physical help, financial support and company for both married men and women.

Robert Marsh and Cheng-Kuang Hsu have studied changing kinship norms and behaviour in Taipei, Taiwan, in comparable surveys conducted in 1963 and 1991 (Marsh and Hsu, 1995). This was a period of time in which Taipei underwent rapid economic growth and population change. They found that normative obligations to kin declined but actual behavioural ties to kin increased. Traditionally, kin would expect each other to conform to a relatively wide range of kinship obligations, which particular members of the extended kin group enforced over other members. From 1963 to 1991 the sense of kinship obligation declined substantially. People in Taipei today feel less obligated to kin to maintain close, intimate relationships, or give respect and obedience, provide economic aid, or help at work and at home. At the same time, however, the actual frequency of getting together with kin has increased. Such occasions as the New Year and ancestor worship had a higher frequency of participation in 1991 than in 1963. Interestingly, more people in the latter year also reported that they had relied on relatives in getting a job or promotion, although this was still relatively uncommon. Thus, normative obligations towards kin have weakened, but actual, behavioural patterns of interaction with kin have increased. Kinship relations cannot be understood as being automatically undermined by the processes of industrialization, modernization and urbanization. The relation between kinship and social change must be interpreted in particular social contexts.

Modernization in Taiwan clearly has had a contradictory effect on kinship ties. Co-residence between parents and adult children has declined, but interaction with kin has increased. Possible reasons for increased interaction with kin include greater ease of travel with more people owning cars, more leisure time with greater affluence, a desire to overcome the effects of social change by returning to one's roots, and increased longevity which facilitates greater contact between the generations. In any event, the high frequency of contact with kin after a period of rapid economic and social change shows that the sentiments upon which kinship ties rest remain strong. Obligations towards kin appear to have changed from formal duties to more voluntaristic bases of action. People maintain relationships with kin because they want to, not because they have to.

DIVORCE

Marriage provides an interesting contrast with kinship. Marriage, too, has become more voluntaristic, as people get married now more because they want to than because of the pressure of social convention. This is witnessed in Western societies by the increased prevalence of cohabitation, which rivals marriage as a basis for the formation of couples in some countries. People also stay married now only because they want to and not because they feel they have to. The norm now is that marriages should be gratifying, not a matter of social obligation or economic necessity. When the family was basically a unit of production, relationships were instrumental. As it became a private sphere of emotional bonds, nurture and affection became the basis for relationships. This meant a loosening up of relationships and a greater priority given to personal gratification. The more importance given to the latter norm in the culture, the less likely people are to remain married when things go wrong. Ending a marriage that no longer works is now a personal choice that is made by many people. Divorce rates increased in the majority of European countries during the 1960s, with the greatest surge occurring after 1970 (Macura *et al.*, 1995). In a study of family change in France, Germany, Quebec and the USA, Howard Bahr, Jean-Hugues Déchaux and Karin Stiehr report that the divorce rate has increased in all four countries since 1960 (Bahr *et al.*, 1994). This result is confirmed in a larger study of family change in 21 industrial nations, including Japan (Chafetz and Hagan, 1996). Divorce is notably high in the contemporary United States, where it has attained a level unmatched by any other modern nation.

Demographers and sociologists predict that, throughout the world, increasing urbanization, industrialization and modernization will lead to rising divorce rates. That is because these factors are related to a number of changes that weaken marriage ties. Modern societies are societies committed to social change intended to bring about progress. As such, they involve turning away from tradition to embrace a better future. Therefore, traditional norms tend to break down with modernization, including reduced social pressure to maintain the marriage relationship. Also, urban-industrial societies create many opportunities for rewarding activities outside family life, and this fosters greater individualism. People are encouraged to pursue their individual interests in an open and competitive social structure. Probably the most widely accepted explanation for rising divorce rates in the West is the decline in the centrality of the family in economic and social matters. There is an increased emphasis on individualism with a greater stress on personal happiness, autonomy and self-realization, with a corresponding increase in the social acceptability of divorce (Jones, 1997). Rather than staying married for the good of the children or to serve the interests of the family, people seek their own interests and happiness and are prepared to look for better opportunities. This includes greatly expanded opportunities for employment, which have had a notable effect on women's lives in recent decades, including the increased economic independence of women. Women's growing capacity for economic autonomy, both through rising labour force participation and through ability to access altered social security provisions for single mothers, has enabled them to live independently. Divorce becomes more feasible to the extent that married women earn, or can earn, their own living. Another factor related to economic change may have been the greater possibility for both sexes to meet potential alternative marriage partners, owing to the movement of more women into the labour force. Greater contact between the sexes at work increases the temptation to engage in extra-marital affairs, increasing the strains on marriage. Finally, it is hypothesized that changing economic and social conditions have increased the levels of stress in family life. For example, both wives and husbands now need to balance the competing commitments of career and family life, which places a greater stress on the marriage relationship. Janet Chafetz and Jacqueline Hagan argue that a major reason for the increased desire to divorce among women is the relative lack of sharing of domestic responsibilities that still characterizes most marriages, and the problems that this creates for employed married women (Chafetz and Hagan, 1996). Wives who are working in jobs as well as in the 'second shift' at home are likely to feel deprived of leisure time relative to their husbands, and this can result in a sense that the social exchange between marriage partners is unequal. Such conflicts become more difficult to resolve as the power resources of husbands and wives become more equal, which is a consequence of the increased employment of married women. Also men's customary authority is eroded by the decline of traditional norms following modernization. The automatic assumption that husbands have the legitimate right to expect compliance from their wives is no longer available as a means of suppressing or resolving conflicts.

The modernization theory of social change and divorce seems to fit Western societies fairly well, but does it fit every society? Gavin Jones has examined this question in a study of trends in divorce in Islamic Southeast Asia and the West (Jones, 1997). He finds that whereas divorce rates have been increasing in the West, among the Muslim populations of Malaysia, Singapore and Indonesia they have actually been decreasing. This has occurred despite rapid urbanization and industrialization associated with economic growth, and increased participation of women in economic activity outside the home. In the 1950s and earlier, divorce rates in Islamic Southeast Asia were at extremely high levels, being several times higher than those in the West. They subsequently fell dramatically, and today they are substantially below Western divorce rates.

The traditional pattern of divorce in Islamic Southeast Asia was one of relatively quick divorce following an arranged marriage between youthful partners who were socially immature. While parent-arranged marriage in the interests of the family was the norm, women were given considerable autonomy and they were not forced to stay in an incompatible marriage. Divorce was generally tolerated and easy to arrange, women had the economic and practical support of their kin upon divorce, including flexible childcare practices, and in societies where polygyny was fairly common wives often avoided its occurrence by seeking a divorce.

Two main factors changed during the period when the Muslim populations of Southeast Asia switched from a high divorce regime to a low divorce regime. Women began marrying at older ages, and there was a trend towards more self-arrangement of marriage. A greater level of social maturity at marriage, combined with a greater personal stake in the success of the marriage, seem to have had a stabilizing effect on marital relationships. The problem with many traditional marriages was that many couples were incompatible from the start, due to the marriage being arranged by parents. Other factors leading to a reduction in divorce have included growing disapproval of divorce and increasingly tight regulations, fuelled by revivalist trends in Islam, and the declining practice of polygyny, which lessened an irritant in traditional marriage. Some of these trends were related to other social and economic developments, including greater influence of the mass media in changing traditional attitudes, rising levels of education, and more employment of young women outside the home.

Clearly, divorce rates have been changing everywhere, but they have not always been changing in the same direction. The underlying factors of change do show some broad similarities, however. This includes the declining influence of tradition, rising levels of education and a greater emphasis on personal autonomy. More personal autonomy in Islamic Southeast Asia has meant a greater choice of marriage partner, and therefore a greater commitment to the marriage relationship. Greater autonomy in the West has been associated with more choice over whether or not to stay married. Another common factor has been economic change, especially the increased employment of women, and its impact on the demand for education.

It has been suggested that the association between modernization and increased divorce in Western societies is due in part to the association between modernization and the changing position of women in society (Fu, 1996). With modernization, the education of women goes up and so does their employment for wages. For example, employment has shifted more towards white-collar occupations and other forms of service work that are more attractive to women. As married women's education increases, and especially as they become employed in greater numbers outside the home, so the possibilities of their being able to survive without their husbands increase. Wives who are not dependent on their husbands become better able to contemplate divorce if the marriage does not work out. Thus, women who would otherwise have been trapped in marriages that they were unable to leave for economic reasons are able to opt out of marriage and stand on their own feet. Women's economic independence, which is closely related to their educational attainment, has been recognized as a key determinant in divorce. For example, Xuanning Fu finds that change in women's education is a strong predictor of change in the divorce rate across a set of 46 nations studied between 1960 and 1990, and this pattern is independent of religious differences (Fu, 1996). As women's education goes up, so too do divorce rates. This finding supports the hypothesis of modernization theories that, over time, improvement in female education raises the divorce rate.

WOMEN AND FAMILY CHANGE

Janet Chafetz and Jacqueline Hagan hypothesize that increases in women's employment and education in recent decades are responsible for several changes in family life, including increased divorce rates (Chafetz and Hagan, 1996). In a sample of 21 industrial nations, they note that although the timing of change varied from country to country, the employment of women has increased everywhere, especially in service occupations. Service occupations have grown dramatically, while manufacturing jobs account for a steadily decreasing proportion of the labour force. Many of these service occupations were sex-typed as female jobs (e.g. clerical work and nursing), and others were new occupations that were similar in type to ones that were already dominated by females (e.g. computer data entry and other health professions). These jobs require a relatively well-educated labour force. More opportunities opened up for better educated women, and growing numbers of women therefore pursued more education. In particular, many more women are now receiving post-secondary education.

One of the consequences of women spending longer in education and needing to spend time establishing their careers is that they have been deferring marriage. Many women, especially the better educated, have combined their commitment to the labour force and their desire for motherhood by postponing the first birth until their education is complete and their careers are well under way. Women have been getting married at older ages as they have made room in their lives for other interests. A related change is that women have been deferring starting a family. Most women still want to have children, but when they do so they are faced with a gender division of labour that continues to assign most of the responsibility for childcare to women. One way out of the contradictory demands of education and employment, and childcare responsibilities, has been to postpone childbearing and to reduce the number of children for whom care is necessary. Age of first birth has increased, and in most nations women have been deferring first birth until at least their late 20s. At the same time, total fertility (total completed family size) has fallen in most countries. Most women in the advanced industrial nations today stop at one or two children, thus enhancing the possibility for them to remain in the labour force. At the same time, social attitudes have changed to reflect changing conditions. Images of the ideal completed family now focus on two children, and stigmas against voluntary childlessness and the one-child family have abated considerably.

THE POSTMODERN FAMILY?

Changing attitudes towards family life in countries like the United States are part of the social phenomenon that Judith Stacey refers to as the post-modern family (Stacey, 1990; 1991). She means by this a period of time in which families are diverse and fluid, and family relations are contested, ambivalent, and undecided. Stacey argues that under postmodern conditions no singular family structure or ideology has arisen to replace the modern family consisting of the nuclear family (an intact married couple with children) with a breadwinner husband and a homemaker wife.

Thanks to the availability of effective contraception, having children is now optional and a matter of personal choice. Whereas many women want to have children, not all do so, and some women decide to remain childfree in order to pursue other interests. Among those interests is the possibility of employment in demanding careers. Women now have a choice over whether to work outside the home or to be homemakers with breadwinner husbands. While many women feel the pressure of economic need and the desire for a high standard of living as reasons for working outside the home, other women are attracted by the ideal of the so-called 'traditional family' (actually what Stacey calls the modern family) with its ideal of female domesticity and the mother as the heart of a child-centred family life. These contrasting images of the preferred form of family life come into conflict over such policy issues as whether or not government programmes for tax relief for childcare costs tend to favour dual-income couples over breadwinner–homemaker couples. There are other conflicts internal to family life.

When women are employed outside the home in jobs that demand their time for many hours of the day, especially if they work full-time, they may seek to renegotiate the division of labour over domestic tasks with their husbands. In general, husbands have not increased the time they spend on housework to a level comparable to the increased time that their wives are employed outside the home, and there is no norma-tive requirement for them to do so. In urban America, husbands do not contribute much to the duties that have traditionally been assigned to wives, despite their wives' changed employment status (Xu, 1998). In contemporary America married women may increasingly participate in the paid labour force, but their husbands do not do much more around the house than do husbands of non-employed wives. This can precipitate conflict over the household division of labour.

Other stresses arise from the increase in divorce. The phenomenon of high levels of divorce means that many individuals must remake their lives, even though society provides no clear script for how to do so. Individuals may remarry and reconstitute something approximating their previous family life. But it is now also perfectly socially acceptable to remain unmarried and, if there are children, to live as a single parent. If individuals remarry, they must then negotiate some arrangement about how they will relate to their ex-spouse, especially when there are children involved. Also, they must re-negotiate relationships with their in-laws, especially grandparents who often have a strong interest in maintaining ties with their grandchildren. This can pose legal issues as well as creating social divisions over such matters as grandparents' rights. The result is a complex array of kinship networks which have become more diverse under conditions of high divorce.

DISCUSSION

Family change is ubiquitous but it does not have a clear pattern of development, and the term 'postmodern family life' best describes the open and undecided character of contemporary family life. On a global scale, it is possible to observe divergence as well as convergence of trends (Xu, 1998). The overall trend is clearly one of individualization, for example in the choice of marriage partner, but contradictory results can be observed. For example, we have noted in Taiwan how the normative bases of interaction with kin have weakened but the frequency of interaction with kin has increased. Industrialization, urbanization and modernization do not necessarily undermine family life, but they do change the content of family relationships. We have seen how in contrast to increased divorce rates in the West, divorce rates have actually declined in Islamic Southeast Asia. Some causal factors are unique to that region, such as the effects of the Islamic revival, but other factors are common such as the increase in free-choice marriage, the role of the mass media in changing attitudes, and the improvements in women's education. The latter factor is thought to have had a particularly important impact on family life, for example in delayed age of marriage and delayed age of bearing a first child. We will look at other demographic changes in more detail in the next chapter.

5 Demographic change

Most people want to have children, and they consider having children as a major means of self-fulfilment (Palomba and Moors, 1995). They enjoy having children around, and they feel that being good parents is one of the greatest satisfactions that life has to offer. However, the value attached to children has been changing. In recent decades, there has been a common pattern of change in key demographic factors in the Western societies. The average number of children born to a woman has fallen, population growth has been correspondingly slower, and we have witnessed increased population ageing (Macura *et al.*, 1995). The driving force behind this change has been falling birth rates. The recent decline in fertility has been brought about especially by a reduction in the number of women having three or more children and, in some countries, by an increase in the prevalence of childlessness. Even in Ireland, which has a history of very high rates of marital fertility, birth rates have fallen dramatically (Murphy-Lawless and McCarthy, 1999). Ireland's demographic regime has converged with that of other modern countries and the total fertility rate is now below the level needed to replace the population, as it is in most of Europe.

CHANGING FERTILITY

Explanations for declining fertility fluctuate between economic explanations and cultural explanations (Beaujot, 1990). Economic explanations include the argument that in some countries the high cost of housing, and poor housing conditions, are indicated as causes of the birth decline (Palomba and Moors, 1995). The main focus, however, is on the costs and benefits of having children. When the family was a unit of production, children provided material benefits to parents through the contribution of their labour to the household economy. Children helped on the farm or in the workshop, and in so doing they helped to provide for themselves. Also, before the emergence of the modern welfare state and economic affluence coupled with financial institutions that permit saving for old age, children were needed to provide for their parents in their declining years. Children therefore had a real value to their parents, and interest in having a number of children was high. John Caldwell has hypothesized that in past societies the net flow of resources was from children to parents (Caldwell, 1976; 1978). This gave parents an economic interest in having many children. That is not the case today.

With modernization, the value of children has declined. Children are now in school, not working, or if they do work they only work part-time for spending money. Also, the welfare state provides pensions and assistance with the needs of daily living for elderly people, and individuals are able to save up for their retirement. Children are no longer needed in old age in the way in which they were needed in the past. At the same time, the costs of having children have increased. Children stay in school or further education longer, and they now remain partly or wholly dependent on their parents for extended periods of time. According to Gary Caldwell, Karin Stiehr, John Modell and Salustiano Del Campo it can be stated with certainty that the decline in fertility since 1960 has been associated with a parallel decline in the proportion of the population with fewer than nine years schooling (Caldwell *et al.*, 1994). As well, interest in the quality of children has risen as parents take their nurturing role more seriously. Expenditures have correspondingly increased on such things as private lessons and equipment like computers that enhance children's learning capacity. In John Caldwell's terms, the net flow of resources is now from parents to children, and it is now economically rational to have fewer children. The costs of having children have also increased in another sense. Taking care of children is time-consuming, and it takes time away from other activities that might be preferred. In particular, it can affect the time that women have for working for wages. This opportunity cost for women has become a major deterrent to having a large family as more women have wanted to earn their own income. There is a wide consensus in the literature on the correlation between declining fertility and increased female labour force participation (Caldwell *et al.*, 1994).

Cultural explanations of falling birth rates emphasize such factors as the declining influence of traditional norms, for example religious norms favouring large numbers of children. Religious authority has waned, and alternative codes of conduct have gained ground. For example, part of the reason for the historically high fertility rate in Ireland was the strong influence of the Roman Catholic Church and its dogmas against contraception and abortion. But as Ireland has developed economically and become urbanized it has also become more secularized. A related factor in fertility change is the growth of individualism and an ethos of self-fulfilment. The 1960s, for example, which witnessed the end of the post-war baby boom, saw a shift towards values of personal self-development. The latter encourages the pursuit of personal interests rather than family or child-centred goals. In some cases people want to remain childless because they do not want to be forced to change their lifestyles. Having children limits freedom of movement, it imposes financial restrictions, and it hampers career plans. The decline in fertility can therefore be interpreted as an expression of the low or negative value placed on children compared with available alternatives.

One of the alternatives to having children is getting a good education. Time spent in education has increased for girls and young women, and this is normally associated with later age of marriage and delayed child-bearing. This, in turn, is related to the increased employment of women and a shift away from an ideology that focused on women only as wives and mothers. Gender-specific roles have been challenged, and women have gained greater autonomy and more control over their lives. This probably means that they now have more influence over reproduction decisions than they had in the past. Italy, for example, is one country in which there has been a considerable change in women's role accompanied by a dramatic decline in fertility (Chesnais, 1996). There has been an enormous expansion in female educational attainment in recent decades, and in the younger birth cohorts girls now have higher average levels of schooling than boys. As a result, young women's expectations and ambitions have changed. No longer satisfied with confinement to the role of wife and mother, they now seek an occupational career with all the financial benefits that brings. Of course, other countries, too, have seen changes in women's roles but without the same dramatic impact on fertility decline. In countries such as France and Sweden public policies have encouraged women to have children by providing considerable financial supports for families with children, and by making it easier for women to combine having children with participation in the paid labour force (Caldwell *et al.*, 1994; Chesnais, 1996). Most Italian women are still committed to traditional marriage, but their solution to the choice they are forced to make between economic well-being and children is often to have fewer children.

Norms concerning the social desirability of marriage appear to be related to fertility patterns. Fertility is still higher for the married than it is for the unmarried, even though there has been a rapid increase in the proportion of births outside marriage since the early 1960s. In general, fewer people have been getting married as more people have been cohabiting or living alone, and this may be a factor that has contributed to the fertility decline in some countries. It is also possible that increased divorce has helped to accelerate the change towards lower fertility. Insofar as children represent an enduring commitment that may outlast marriage, they may come to be seen as a burden in societies with high divorce rates. Thus people may be having fewer children in order to avoid commitments to relationships that may not last. People who do not want children sometimes explain their intentions on the basis of the fact that they do not have a stable relationship (Palomba and Moors, 1995).

Another factor is that the cultural norms surrounding family size and sexuality have changed. Women are no longer expected to have many children, and they may be considered irresponsible if they do. This is associated with the legitimation of sexual activity that is not aimed at procreation, first inside marriage and later outside marriage. Of course, all of this is predicated on the availability of effective contraception, so that women can now control their fertility in a way that was not possible in earlier generations. Widespread availability of the Pill, in particular, is thought to have played a major role in declining birth rates. For example, part of the explanation for the dramatic decline in fertility in Ireland is accounted for by the opening up of legal access to contraception. Legal access to contraceptives and to information about contraception was severely limited in Ireland after the founding of the Irish State in 1922, but was finally modified beginning in the late 1970s. The idea of limiting births within marriage, and the use of contraception, are cultural innovations whose legitimacy has spread over time. The conscious regulation of births by married couples represents a new model of behaviour that has spread around the world, partly by the deliberate efforts of agencies interested in population control and other public policies, and partly through the normal mechanisms of cultural diffusion such as the mass media. In Ireland, for example, the women's movement played a leading role in agitating for the removal of restrictions on the availability of contraception, and it therefore contributed to that country's fertility decline (Murphy-Lawless and McCarthy, 1999).

POPULATION AGEING

Fertility decline, together with increased longevity, has led to growing proportions of older people in the populations of many countries. This phenomenon of population ageing has implications for family relationships and for social policies. Japan is one nation that is experiencing rapid population ageing due to rapid decline in fertility and mortality (Hashimoto and Takahashi, 1995; Ogawa and Retherford, 1997;

Koyano, 1999). The fertility rate has fallen well below the replacement level, and more people are surviving into old age and living longer. Japan is now one of the most aged of the developed countries, and it is projected that the proportion of the population aged 65 and older will rise to unprecedented levels. In particular, due to an exceptionally high life expectancy, Japan has a relatively high proportion of the 'old old' (75+) among the elderly. The significance of the 'old old' is that they place especially heavy burdens on families and the health-care system. This poses a challenge of adjustment for families and for government policy makers alike.

One of the problems arising from population ageing is how to provide care for the growing numbers of disabled elderly who need assistance with the needs of daily living. Traditionally, this was provided through co-residence with a family member who provided care. Institutional care was regarded as a disgrace for it was taken as an explicit sign of an unsuccessful family life. However, family life in Japan has been changing (Morioka, 1996). Historically, the preferred form of financial support and care for elderly parents was for them to live in a stem family with the eldest son and his wife. Living in the same household, the elderly person was given every kind of support by the successor, his wife, and their children. Before the end of the Second World War this was a legal obligation as well as a social obligation, and it was exclusively the family that ensured the care of the elderly. This was reinforced by norms of filial piety, in which children were seen as owing feelings of gratitude and respect towards their parents in return for the things they had received from them when they were young. Filial piety was regarded as an extremely important moral virtue that was the subject of explicit instruction.

After the war, the legal obligation to co-reside with elderly parents was removed. However, social norms of co-residence remained strong for two decades, and are still stronger than they are in the West (Hashimoto, 1996). Beginning in the 1960s, co-residence between parents and children began to decline and the numbers of older people living alone or just with their spouse began to rise. In particular, although eldest sons are much more likely than other sons to co-reside with their parents, the value favouring co-residence with the eldest son has weakened considerably over time. Co-residence has continued decreasing although it remains high by Western standards, and it is expected to decrease further. Part of the reason for this shift was that public pensions became effective in the 1960s, and the attitude began to develop that parents should not be dependent upon their children. Expectations of old-age support from children have declined greatly over time. Also, urbanization and greater geographical mobility, and more education, have loosened ties between parents and children.

The decline in co-residence has led to difficulties in the provision of care for disabled elderly parents. Another contributing factor to this problem has been the increased labour force participation of women. Caring for the elderly may conflict with work outside the home, as the opportunity costs of caring are high in terms of forgone wages during the period of care. Family caregivers for the elderly in Japan tend to be middle-aged women. Since caring for the elderly can conflict with work outside the home, the rising labour force participation rate of middle-aged women may affect the ability of families to care for the elderly. Fewer daughters and daughters-in-law may be available to provide continuous care for their parents in the home. Perhaps for this reason, perhaps for other reasons, the value attached to children caring for their elderly parents has declined. These changes have implications for public policy intended to cope with the problems of population ageing. Decline in co-residence, increases in women's education and full-time paid employment, and weakening values of filial piety all suggest a continuing decline in the ability and willingness of families in Japan to provide care for the elderly. As a result of all of these changes, and stimulated by the prospect of a growing proportion of the population who are older and in need of support and care, the Japanese government has been wrestling with the pressures of population ageing.

Another country which is adjusting to population ageing as a result of increased life expectancy and a falling birth rate is Korea. Korea has experienced a major demographic transition from high fertility and high mortality to low fertility and low mortality. Rapid socioeconomic development, combined with the full-scale adoption of family planning programmes, facilitated the demographic transition in Korea. After the beginning of the 1960s, it went from a rapidly growing population to a moderately growing one (Kim, 1999). As a result, there has been a substantial increase in both the proportion and the absolute number of the elderly, and they are projected to increase much more in the future (Choi, 1996). The speed of the population ageing process in Korea is faster than that of the developed countries, as a result of the abrupt onset of the demographic transition.

As in Japan, responses to population ageing have been complicated by accompanying social changes. Socioeconomic development, including massive migration from the rural areas to the cities, has resulted in the decline of the traditional stem family. As a result, there has been a sharp decrease in the proportion of elderly people living with their children, and a corresponding increase in the proportion of the elderly living alone or with their spouse, especially in the rural areas. The rate of urbanization for the older population has been lower than that for the population as a whole, and out-migration of the young from the rural areas has left many older people living on their own. Declining co-residence between the generations may also be due to a desire to avoid intergenerational conflict. The elderly and their children often have different value orientations as a result of different social experiences, including different educational levels.

Recent changes affect the level of support and care that the elderly receive from their children, as financial support, emotional support, and assistance with activities, etc. are all higher with co-residence. Although the proportion of the elderly receiving financial support from family members remains high, older people living alone often suffer from serious economic problems. Many Korean elderly assume that they will receive financial assistance from their children; however, such support is not always available due to recent social changes. Due to the combination of population ageing and social change, an increasing number of Korean elderly will likely suffer from financial difficulties because of their children's avoidance or inability to provide financial support. One of the most serious aspects of the ageing problem in Korea is economic insecurity.

Norms about support and care for the elderly by their children in Korea were traditionally strong, and they appear to remain relatively strong. Nevertheless, traditional patterns of co-residence are eroding and are likely to be affected by further changes. It is a dilemma for Korea whether the growing numbers of elderly should be supported and cared for by the family or by the government. So far, the main responsibility has been taken by the family. Despite the forces of industrialization and urbanization, Korean families still provide the major part of old-age support and caregiving. Since women are the dominant caregivers, this means that the burden of caregiving carried by women is increasing (Suh, 1994). This burden will be particularly heavy for daughters-in-law, who still play the role of most important caregiver for elderly people. Problems may arise here in the future, as the rate of women's participation in occupational activities has increased and is likely to go on increasing. This pattern tends to make it difficult to care for the elderly within the family, as women are expected to bear the caring role according to cultural tradition.

DISCUSSION

The relative stability of traditional gender roles in Japan contrasts sharply with the rapidity of demographic change in that country. Clearly, specific social changes and demographic changes need not occur at the same rate. In this chapter we have seen that demographic change is related to social change in two ways. First, social change causes demographic change. We have looked at this issue especially with reference to fertility declines in the Western societies. Increased education, for example, changes the balance of costs and benefits for children as children do less productive work and they cost more to support for longer periods of time. It therefore becomes rational to have fewer children. Also, more education raises expectations and ambitions, especially among women, and it increases women's interest in alternatives to domesticity and motherhood. Changes in education are therefore a factor in changing fertility decisions. Increased education in turn is related to other social changes such as industrialization, as industrialized societies both require and provide more opportunities for educated workers.

The second relationship between demographic change and social change is that the effects of demographic change are filtered through patterns of social change. We have looked at this aspect of demographic change with special reference to population ageing, focusing on the societies of Japan and Korea. These two societies are going through very significant population ageing due to declining fertility and increased longevity. This poses challenges for families and governments as they try to cope with the increasing numbers of elderly who are in need of support and care. In Japan and Korea much discussion of the effects of this change has focused on declining co-residence between adult children and their elderly parents, although rates of intergenerational co-residence remain high there by Western criteria. Traditionally, rates of co-residence were very high and provided the context for most support and caregiving. With economic and social change, however, rates of co-residence are declining. For example, urbanization with its flow of mostly young people from rural areas to urban areas often separates the generations. Also, economic development has provided more occupational opportunities for women, which can mean that fewer women are available to provide continuous care for elderly parents within the home. Work, and its economic rewards, figures prominently in recent changes affecting family life.

6 Family, work and money

Work can be divided into paid and unpaid work. The division between paid and unpaid work continues to reflect gender roles, despite all the changes that have occurred in recent decades. Men tend to spend more time on paid work than women, but women tend to spend more time on unpaid work than men (Devereaux, 1993; Haas, 1999; Walker, 1999). The kinds of unpaid activities in which women and men engage also differ. In the United States, for example, men spend more time than women on household repairs, home-management and obtaining services for the family (Robinson and Godbey, 1997). Women, on the other hand, spend more time than men on the core housework activities of cooking, cleaning and laundry, and on childcare. Husbands tend to do tasks that are done relatively infrequently, such as painting the house, whereas wives tend to do tasks that are done more frequently, such as clothes washing. Men spend very little time on average in doing traditionally female tasks. Women also spend more time than men on childcare, even when they work full-time. In such cases it is mainly the mother who makes arrangements for the care of the child during working hours, and who takes the child to and from the childcare location. Once home with the child, it is the mother who has the main responsibility for the child, although the husband may assist her.

HOUSEHOLD WORK

The amount of time spent on housework varies not only by gender but also by marital status – at least it does for women. In the United States, Scott South and Glenna Spitze have compared married persons with those who either never married and are living in the parental household, or never married and are living independently, or cohabiting, or divorced or separated, or widowed (South and Spitze, 1994). They found that married women do the most housework and never-married men living in the parental household do the least. The latter are closely followed by married men, who do much less housework than their wives. Married women perform significantly more housework than women in the other five statuses, with the biggest difference being between married women and women who reside in the parental household. Among men, on the other hand, differences in hours worked in housework by marital status are comparatively small. Married men do significantly more housework than never-married men who still live with their parents, and significantly less than divorced or widowed men, but these differences are modest compared with those for women. Also, while the presence of children in the household creates more housework, the impact of children on housework hours tends to be significantly stronger for women than for men.

In all marital statuses women spend more hours on housework than men. This gender gap is even found among those who never married and are living with their parents, who perform the least amount of housework. Never-married women and men who live independently do more housework than the never-married who remain at home, but the increase is slightly greater for women than for men. Presumably, both men and women who live independently do household tasks that had previously been done for them by their parents. The gender difference in time spent on housework widens when women live with a partner, but especially when they are married. Cohabiting women do considerably more housework than cohabiting men, but the gender gap in time spent on housework reaches its peak among married women and men.

South and Spitze argue that their findings are to be explained by the conventional implications of 'doing gender' in marriage. Gender is constructed through the everyday tasks of daily living, which follow a gender script of culturally inscribed roles. Men expect, and are expected, to be dominant in marriage, and as such they do fewer of the household tasks, which are left to their wives to perform. Women do gender in marriage by performing housework for their husbands as a way of showing them that they love them. They incorporate the idea that housework is women's work into their own self-image, and they attempt to demonstrate that they are good wives by providing satisfactory housework (Ferree, 1991b). Some women, at least, are committed to an internalized standard of achievement according to which doing housework reflects creditably on them as women and as wives. The more an employed wife cares about a clean house, having a proper dinner on the table and maintaining the same standards of housework as if she were not employed, the fewer conventionally female chores her husband does.

EMPLOYMENT AND HOUSEWORK

The finding that the amount of housework men do varies little by marital status is paralleled by the finding that the amount of housework done by husbands does not vary much according to whether their wives are employed or not. A review of the literature in the United States by Myra Marx Ferree finds that men whose wives are employed spend little more time on housework and childcare than men with non-employed wives (Ferree, 1991a). A review of the literature in Britain by Jane Pilcher comes to a similar conclusion (Pilcher, 1999). The most egalitarian arrangements for unpaid work are found in dual-career couples where both partners work full-time, yet even here women tend to do more household work and childcare than men. In such cases, women's total workload is more than men's. Wives with full-time jobs work longer per day than their husbands do, and despite the amount of time spent in employment they maintain much more domestic responsibility than their husbands (Gershuny, 1992).

As an extension of the finding that dual-career families in which both partners work full-time have more egalitarian arrangements for unpaid work than families with different work patterns, Tracey Warren has found in Britain that women who are employed in manual jobs contribute a proportionally higher share of caring work than do women who are employed in professional jobs, mainly because the former are more likely to work part-time (Warren, 2003). Women in professional couples still live in families in which it is women who do most of the caring, but their workload is eased in two ways. First, professional women are more likely to buy in domestic services to replace some of their domestic labour, reflecting their better financial position. The services which are most likely to be purchased are cleaning and childcare. Second, the spouses of women who are employed in professional jobs do participate in certain household tasks. However, the contributions of these men are modest, and they do not alter the fact that they are still living in predominantly female-carer couples. The major exception to this pattern was found among men in working-class couples where the husband and wife worked split schedules. Here, the men participated to a significant extent in caring for their children, and more than professional men, perhaps because these working-class families could not afford to hire child-minders.

Jane Pilcher notes that although men with employed partners do more household work than those without, the most striking reality is that employed wives do most of this work. She further notes that when men are unemployed they do increase their participation in household tasks, but not enough to constitute a fundamental challenge to the established pattern in which women do most of the housework. The only situation in which that pattern may be effectively challenged, Pilcher observes, is for women with a relatively high-class position. It seems that there is a class division in the relationship between employment and household work in Britain. Women in higher-status, professional and relatively well-paid occupations may face less inequitable distributions of household work than women in relatively low-status, semi- or unskilled and relatively poorly paid occupations because the former hire the latter to help them with their domestic work. Apparently, one potential solution to men's continued reluctance to take on much additional domestic work is to hire someone else to do it, especially in the areas of childcare for pre-school children and household cleaning. There has been a surge in demand for these services, particularly from middle-class households with both partners in full-time professional occupations. However, the performance of domestic labour remains a gendered phenomenon, as it is mainly women who provide these services. The employment of waged domestic labour amounts to female partners buying in the labour of other women to undertake the housework and childcare that their husbands decline to do.

In Sweden, this solution has been unavailable for ideological reasons, as it is predicated upon an assumption of class inequality which is contrary to public policy in that country (Sandqvist, 1992). As a result, there has been greater pressure upon men to participate in household work in order to relieve their employed wives. An ideology of gender equality has taken root that holds that men and women should perform equal roles within the family. The equal roles family paradigm maintains that both husband and wife should be equally responsible for earning money, they should have equal opportunities to pursue a career and they should be equally responsible for housework and childcare. Since equal opportunities in paid employment requires the availability of both women and men for full-time work, childcare outside the home is necessary for the system to work.

Female labour force participation is high in Sweden, including mothers of young children; however, female parents are more likely to reduce their hours of paid employment than male parents. In response to this pattern of employment, Swedish fathers have become more involved in household work, especially if their wives are employed full-time. Contemporary fathers are more involved in housework and take on much more responsibility for the care of young children than men did in the past. However, the division of tasks between husbands and wives still tends to follow traditional gender divisions, even in Sweden.

By comparison, it seems that in countries like Britain and the United States men resist doing much extra housework whatever the position of their partners, or themselves. It therefore follows that the rapid expansion of married women's labour force participation in recent decades has not been accompanied by a similar growth in the amount of work done by men at home. Women, especially mothers, and especially mothers of young children, have been increasing their participation in the paid labour force (Menaghan and Parcel, 1990; Brannen and Moss, 1998). Clearly, women's paid employment has been changing. But men have generally not responded by raising their contribution to work done at home to match that of their wives. However, change does seem to be occurring slowly, as an apparently growing proportion of dual-earner couples are in relatively egalitarian arrangements (Menaghan and Parcel, 1990; Ferree, 1991b; Gershuny, 1992). Whether or not husbands give priority to equality in housework is particularly associated with their participation, and more husbands now believe that housework should be an equal responsibility. The amount of time that men spend in unpaid work has been increasing, but the husbands of employed wives still do the smaller proportion of the household's total work. Women's increased participation in paid work has been only partly offset by men's increased participation in unpaid work. Even when the share of housework husbands contribute is shown to rise with their wives' employment, this is more because the amount of time spent by employed wives on housework falls than because the amount of time spent by their husbands increases. Women who work more hours per week are more likely to lower their personal standards for housework, and as a result the total amount of housework contributed to the domestic economy drops. The amount of housework done by men with employed wives therefore appears to increase in relative importance, even though there has been relatively little change in the absolute amount of work that they do.

EMPLOYMENT AND FAMILY RESPONSIBILITIES

The fact that men have not substantially increased their time spent on domestic chores has made it more difficult for employed women to integrate a career with motherhood. The fact that women, in general, continue to assume the primary responsibility for childcare and other household tasks affects their choice of occupations, their time spent in paid employment, their work commitment, and their allocation of effort to household and workplace activities. Nevertheless, employment has increased faster among women with children than it has among women without children, and among women with children it has increased more among mothers with young children than it has increased among mothers with older children (Harrop and Moss, 1995).

With the arrival of children, women's limited supply of time has to be allocated between increased household work and employment activities. Children and employment impose competing demands on mothers, and there are strong normative pressures to give priority to the children, especially in the first year of life. Being a mother therefore has an impact on women's employment. Upon giving birth, many women withdraw from the labour force either temporarily or permanently. When they return to work they may return either to full-time work or part-time work. Women in higher powered occupations are the most likely to return to work before their child's first birthday (Saurel-Cubizolles *et al.*, 1999). This may be in part because of the greater career disadvantages of prolonged absence from the workplace in higher powered occupations, and women with better jobs probably have more long-term career plans. Work satisfaction may also be a factor, as women working in higher powered occupations probably have more interesting jobs with lower physical demands. Women who are not satisfied with their job at the time of giving birth are less likely to return to work before the baby's first birthday.

Part-time employment is one strategy that many women have adopted to help them balance the need for earned income with family responsibilities. In Britain, for example, more women with children have part-time jobs than do women without children (Harrop and Moss, 1995). However, the prevalence of part-time work varies from one country to another. For example, part-time work plays a very important role in enabling women to combine childcare with employment in Germany, but it plays a lesser role in the United States where more mothers work full-time (Drobnic, 2000). The prevailing norms concerning employment of mothers differ substantially between the two countries. Germans are the least supportive of women engaging in paid employment when they have small children, whereas Americans are much more supportive of women working whatever the circumstances. Not surprisingly, having children has a stronger impact on the employment patterns of women in Germany than in America. The presence of pre-school children has a dampening effect on full-time employment in both countries, but the effect is stronger for German women than for American women (Drobnic *et al.*, 1999). The presence of a pre-school child moderately increases the risk of leaving full-time employment in the United States, but in Germany there is a greater propensity for mothers of young children to leave full-time employment. Also, mothers of pre-schoolers are less likely than childless women to enter full-time employment after an employment interruption.

Part-time work is an important form of re-employment after having children among German women, especially if they are married. In contrast, the likelihood of entering part-time employment in the US depends little on a woman's family situation. In Germany, part-time work seems to be used systematically as a strategy to combine employment and child-rearing, whereas that is not the case in the United States. Part-time jobs, a typical employment choice for married German women, provide a supplementary income in families where husbands are the main bread-winners. In contrast, single mothers in Germany rely more on full-time employment than married mothers do. It seems that part-time employment is a prevalent option for re-entering the labour market for married women, whereas single mothers opt for full-time employment when their children reach school age. Presumably this is because the latter do not have a husband's income to share, and so they have relatively greater income earning needs.

ECONOMIC POSITION OF SINGLE MOTHERS

Women who are not married do not have direct access to the income of a man, as married women do. As a result, single motherhood is a major cause of poverty among women, and families headed by single mothers are over-represented among the poor. Single mothers have relatively great income needs, since they have children to provide for, but they receive only limited financial support, if any, from the father since he does not live with them. Furthermore, single mothers are disadvantaged insofar as women tend to earn lower wages than men (Menaghan and Parcel, 1990). However, there are national differences in the severity of the economic problems faced by single mothers. For example, Sweden is one country where women's wages are relatively high compared with men's. Also, the Swedish state provides significant economic support in the form of provision for childcare for employed mothers and public income transfers for single mothers in particular. Consequently, in Sweden the economic problems of single mothers are relatively minor. In contrast, the United States is a country where women's wages are somewhat lower relative to men's than in Sweden, and the state does less to help single mothers meet their high income needs. As a result, the economic position of single mothers is more severe there (Sorensen, 1994). The situation in Germany falls somewhere between that in Sweden and the United States, although the difference between the United States and Germany is relatively small. In Sweden, single mothers have lower incomes on average than married mothers, but few of them are poor. In the United States and Germany single mothers have lower incomes and a higher proportion of them are poor. Single mothers in the United States and Germany must therefore make hard choices about how to make ends meet, and how to allocate their time between paid employment and caring for their children.

BALANCING WORK AND FAMILY

Employment on one hand, and housework and childcare on the other hand, constitute competing commitments which mean that many women must make difficult choices about how to allocate their time. Should they spend more time on employment and less time on housework and child-care, by lowering standards of household cleanliness and tidiness for example, or by reducing family size or forgoing childbearing entirely? Or should they spend more time on housework and childcare and less time on employment, by working part-time or by withdrawing from the labour force completely? These choices can be made in many different ways. The reality is one of variability in the extent and meaning of women's and men's paid and unpaid work, and the choices made between them (Ferree, 1991a). Behavioural averages, such as those considered earlier in this chapter, hide this variability. However, it is in the variations in behaviour that we see the clearest signs of change.

Kathleen Gerson has studied the choices made between paid and unpaid work by women in the United States (Gerson, 1991). Apparently, early socialization experiences make little difference to later life course trajectories, as women's initial role orientations are flexible and responsive to changing circumstances. Gerson finds that orientations towards occupational career and domesticity in childhood have relatively little influence on the choices that women make in adulthood. Rather, she concludes that women decide between domestic and non-domestic allocations of time according to the influence upon them of structural constraints and opportunities. Women opt for a life with a career at the centre, or they subordinate their employment goals to motherhood and family activities, according to the package of opportunities and constraints that they face.

Women tend to develop stronger occupational commitments if they experience marital instability and an unsatisfactory relationship with their husband, or if they are disillusioned with housework and mother-hood because they are experienced as relatively isolating and under-valued, and because they are seen as unfulfilling compared with the rewards of paid work. The rewards of paid work are found to be especially valuable if there is a severe economic squeeze in the house-hold, which the wife's earnings help to overcome. Under such conditions, women are likely to feel that they make a significant contribution to the household economy, which entitles them to some redefinition of household tasks. Wives who are breadwinners are significantly more likely to feel entitled to help at home, and in general they are also more likely to receive it (Ferree, 1991a). Pay equity and other structural changes such as women's increased education enable women to earn wages more comparable to men's and are leading to changing perceptions among women of themselves as breadwinners. This in turn is likely to encourage a stronger non-domestic orientation. Women are also more likely to develop a non-domestic orientation if they have chances for advancement at the workplace which provide them with the experience of career mobility. According to Kathleen Gerson, exposure to unanticipated opportunities outside the home, together with unexpected disappointment in domestic pursuits, combine to encourage a non-domestic approach even among those who had initially planned for a married life of domesticity.

On the other hand, women are more likely to allocate their time to domestic responsibilities if they have a stable marriage with a satisfactory relationship with their husband, and the husband has a secure career that enables him to support his wife financially. This has special implications for the domestic division of labour if women's earning power is low. Not all women are able, or willing, to assume the long-term obligation of earning a major portion of the essential income for their families. Under such conditions, wives' earnings are defined as relatively less essential, and hence pose less of a challenge to the division of roles between husband as breadwinner and wife as homemaker. When husbands are financially dominant and deeply involved with their jobs, it is their wives who adjust to meet the family's needs, by shifting their work aspirations to accommodate their definition as homemakers first and foremost. Husbands who care deeply about their work tend to resist any reallocation of tasks at home, probably because they judge that taking on such responsibilities would handicap them in their pursuit of career advancement.

Women are also more likely to follow a domestic orientation if they find that motherhood provides a more satisfying pattern of activity than paid work. If they fear that time spent in paid employment will take them away from their children then they may resist involvement in shared breadwinning. Women are particularly likely to find motherhood more satisfying if their experiences of employment have been in dead-end jobs with little opportunity for advancement. According to Kathleen Gerson, when the experience of blocked mobility at the workplace is combined with unexpected marital commitment to a securely employed

spouse, even women who once held career aspirations are encouraged
to loosen their employment ties and turn towards domestic pursuits.
Recent increases in the insecurity of marriage, and improved career
opportunities for women, have, however, made this a less attractive
option for many women today.

The increasing numbers of married women who opt for employment
rather than domesticity must still somehow combine their family
responsibilities with their responsibilities to their employers. They do so
in several ways. One strategy for balancing paid work and household
work is to have fewer children, or to give up having children entirely.
This strategy is sometimes adopted because of the high expectations of
employers, or because of the high aspirations of employees. Taking time
off for family issues such as childbirth and the care of sick children
can be difficult when doing so means losing out on opportunities for
advancement and being out of touch with office politics. Another strategy is to re-evaluate childcare, by developing new ideologies about
mothering. Thus, there may be an emphasis on spending 'quality time'
with the child in the time away from work rather than simply being
available throughout the day. Finally, mothers who are committed to
employment may try to get their partners to take on more of the burden
of childcare. In particular, wives who bring in a substantial portion
of the family income are more likely to be able to renegotiate who does
the household work. Under such conditions, both spouses tend to accept
the wife's entitlement to a more equal division of labour at home, and
husbands take on more responsibility for children and chores, in that
order. Fathers have faced increasing pressures to be involved in their
children's lives, and some men have responded in positive ways. The
model of man as the primary breadwinner who emphasizes economic
support and limited participation in child-rearing still exists, but it is no
longer as popular as it once was.

Change in men's lives, while relatively limited, is nonetheless part of
overall family change. Some men, of course, have shifted away from
family commitments by remaining single or childless, or by weakening
their ties to their offspring following divorce. Other men, however, have
become more involved in the caring work of family life. Such men do not
usually assume equal responsibility for child-rearing, but they are
nevertheless significantly more involved than their fathers were. Again,
Kathleen Gerson concludes that men's choices about whether or not to
become involved in childcare are the results of structural constraints and
opportunities.

Men who have rewarding and demanding jobs, and who have a stable
relationship with a domestically oriented wife, are likely to take on the

role of a primary breadwinner who is relatively uninvolved in childcare, even if that was not their original inclination. These men emphasize their financial contributions to their families rather than the time they spend on family life. They stress the importance of being a good provider who provides financial support rather than participating in child-rearing, even when their wives are employed. Historically, women have been expected to contribute supplemental earnings to their families, and that remains the pattern in many families today. Here, women's incomes are defined as being of secondary importance, both by comparison with men's incomes and by comparison with women's domestic responsibilities. On the other hand, men who experience employment instability or who find themselves dissatisfied with the pressures of working in rule-governed bureaucracies have a different approach. Such men view breadwinning responsibilities as burdensome and constricting, and they may move in one of two directions.

If men with weak commitments to paid work experience unstable relationships with women and unsatisfactory encounters with children then they may avoid parental involvement altogether, by remaining childless or by weakening their ties to children after divorce. These men typically value autonomy over commitment, and they see children as a threat to their freedom of choice. If, however, weak commitments to paid work are coupled with a stable marital relationship and unexpected pleasure in interactions with children, then men tend to move in the direction of involved fatherhood. In contrast to childless men, these men place family at the centre of their lives, and they value spending time with their families as much as contributing money to them. This pattern is especially likely if their wives have a strong commitment to paid work. The time constraints on their wives and their wives' relatively large financial contributions to the household economy combine to promote a relationship with relatively little role segregation. Here there is a more equal emphasis on sharing both the earning of income and child-rearing. While complete equality remains rare, even among dual-career couples, male participation in childcare is nevertheless on the rise. Such men help their employed wives to look after the children, thus enabling their wives to reduce their burden of responsibilities.

Involved fathers, like employed mothers, juggle the conflicting demands of employment and fatherhood. They may do this by cutting back on overtime, or by using their vacation time to care for sick children. Some men may even prefer to become full-time homemakers. However, that is rarely possible since men's wages remain essential to the lifestyles of the vast majority of households, and few couples are comfortable with an arrangement in which a woman supports a man.

Even when a man wishes to be a more involved father, he is rarely able to trade full-time employment for full-time parenting. More likely is a situation in which both husband and wife try to maintain equal commitments to both paid employment and domestic responsibilities. Rosanna Hertz has studied these couples in the United States (Hertz, 1999).

Couples who share equally in parenting and employment are found in one of two situations, according to Hertz. On one hand, there are couples in which both spouses have middle-managerial or professional positions and who hold the belief that equal parental contributions to child-rearing constitute a superior strategy to purchasing childcare in the marketplace. They believe that men and women should both work outside and inside the home and share the responsibility for child-rearing. The nature of the jobs held by these couples enables them to request more flexible work time or fewer workdays from their employers. Because of their importance to the company, and because their jobs involve a fair amount of working autonomy anyway, their requests are likely to be met with a sympathetic response. This solution to the pressures of combining employment and family responsibilities is especially likely to be found where workers can suggest that they be evaluated on the basis of tasks completed rather than time spent in the workplace. Shifting the work culture to performance evaluation as apart from employee visibility allows employees to structure their own work schedules and pace of work. For example, it may allow them to take afternoons off to coach sports teams or chauffeur children to enrichment activities.

The other situation in which we may find a relatively egalitarian balance of employment and family responsibilities in the contemporary United States is when blue collar husbands are underemployed or are able to adjust their shifts to accommodate their family commitments. Here, fathers may spend more time with their children because they find themselves involuntarily spending less time in the workplace. These men are typically workers whose jobs have been affected by economic restructuring. They are forced to piece together new employment and childcare arrangements from which more active fathering is a by-product. Alternatively, there are couples who both work shifts and who are able to arrange them so that they work at different times of day, thus enabling them to provide continuous childcare at home.

In contrast, workers who do not create a more balanced arrangement of employment and family responsibilities tend to be found in jobs that are very demanding or relatively inflexible. At the higher occupational level, there are people at, or close to, the top of organizations who have great responsibility for supervising the work of others. These workers are extremely reluctant to give up salient parts of their careers in order to redefine their work and family goals, and they are among the least likely to restructure their employment. At a lower occupational level, there are workers who are governed by inflexible rules concerning the nature of their work time, and who are not sufficiently important to the company that they have any leverage in negotiating special arrangements. Here, men are unlikely to be able to shift their work patterns to respond to the conflicting demands of husbands' and wives' employment and family responsibilities.

DISCUSSION

The impact of women's increased employment on family life has been a major subject of concern in recent years. We have seen this here in several issues. Of greatest concern has been the question of how far men have adjusted their roles as husbands and fathers to accommodate their wives' increased commitments outside the home. The findings are contradictory. On one hand, there is evidence of change in some men's family activities in response to their wives' employment. On the other hand, there is evidence that women still carry the greater burden of household work despite being employed, even when they work full-time. A secondary concern has been the extent to which women adjust their employment to help them meet the demands of their family commitments. For example, they may work part-time rather than full-time as a strategy for balancing employment and family life. Or, they may work alternate shifts with their partners in order to enable them to provide continuous childcare. Whatever the strategy, families need to find some way of balancing their economic activities with their caregiving functions.

7 Caring

Caring, or caregiving, refers to intervention on behalf of a dependent person as a result of some requirement of moral behaviour (Leira, 1994). This moral obligation may be public, as in the obligation of the state to provide a duty of care to its citizens, or it may be private, as in the commitment of family members to provide care for one another. The balance between public and private care varies from one society to another, with the public provision of care being notably high in the Scandinavian societies, and the private provision of care being notably high in the Asian societies. Some private provision of care is found in every society, however. The advanced welfare state in Scandinavia, for example, has not made personal moral obligations redundant. Welfare state legislation and provisions define a considerable share of the vitally necessary care for children and the elderly as a private concern.

Private caregiving originates in a social relationship in which one person cares about another. Caring about someone may be a result of feelings of love towards that person, or it may be the result of feelings of duty that arise from social expectations about the roles that people occupy with respect to one another. Either way, the caregiver is motivated to help meet the needs of someone who is unable to meet all of their needs on their own. He or, usually, she recognizes and interprets the situation of the person who is not able to care for themselves, which involves a mental preparedness to receive the message that care is needed. Sometimes these commitments arise from local norms about family relationships, and sometimes they arise from the dynamics of personal relationships.

Janet Finch has studied caregiving obligations in England and she has found that there is little agreement there on the nature of the obligations that adult children have towards their elderly parents (Finch, 1995). The majority of people say that children have an obligation to look after their parents when they are old, but a substantial minority do not. Interestingly, older people in her study were less likely than younger respondents to say that children have a responsibility to care for their parents. Overall, English people seem to prefer that responsibility for the elderly should not fall on the family, but if it has to be the family that provides care then among the available relatives it should be children who do so (Finch and Mason, 1990a). However, although people generally see it as appropriate that adult children should do something to support their parents, there is less agreement about what exactly children should do. The only strong agreements were that daughters are rarely chosen as the appropriate people to provide financial support, and sons are rarely chosen as the people who should provide care for an elderly woman. There is a tendency to prefer that intimate care should be provided by a child of the same sex, particularly where this involves physical touching.

The evidence suggests that norms about caring for parents in England are only weakly developed. There is agreement that children should do something to assist their parents (though this is by no means universal), but it is not always clear what they should do, or who should do it, or what limits might apply to filial obligation. The decision to provide care depends upon the circumstances of the case. Actual caregiving tends to be a result of commitments between particular persons that are built up over a lifetime of social interaction. These commitments develop through contact, through shared activities, and particularly through each giving the other help when and as it is needed. It is above all the process of reciprocity involved in giving and receiving help which is responsible for the development of commitments to care. Those who receive help feel obliged to provide it in return in the future. Therefore, one important reason why some children develop much stronger commitments to their parents than others is that their life circumstances have meant that they had a greater need to call on their parents for assistance, and their parents were in a position to supply help.

Responsibilities arrived at in this way differ from one child to another depending on the dynamics of their relationships, rather than reflecting a universal set of moral guidelines for relations between parents and children. Here, it is the quality of the particular relationship that accounts for the strength of the responsibility to care. Responsibilities are commitments which build up over time between certain parents and certain children, instead of being obligations which flow simply from being an adult child with an aged parent. Janet Finch notes that an implication of this pattern is that the conflict between paid employment and family caregiving that is thought to exist for many women today affects some women, but not all.

PAID EMPLOYMENT AND PRIVATE CARE

One of the issues that is sometimes thought to confront families today is the reduced availability of women to provide care due to their increased employment. This is an issue especially because women spend significantly more hours than men in caregiving (Pyper, 2006). Women who work for wages, especially if they work full-time, simply have less free time available which they can reallocate for family caregiving. If their parents need intensive care they may therefore be caught in a bind. Should they give up their jobs in order to provide care for an elderly parent, or should they keep their jobs and leave their parents to make alternative arrangements?

Providing care may affect participation in paid employment, but equally a potential carer's employment status may affect the likelihood of their becoming a carer and the nature of care that is provided. Janet Finch concludes from her research that contemporary Britons are more likely to favour a woman giving up her job to care for an elderly parent if there is a history of significant mutual support between them. In another study in Britain, daughters who expressed the most satisfaction with their experience of caring for their mothers were those whose relationships with them had previously been supportive and largely remained so (Lewis and Meredith, 1988). Nevertheless, only a minority of Britons favour a woman giving up her employment in order to care (Finch and Mason, 1990c).

There is little evidence that women who are employed at the time when a relative needs care see it as appropriate to give up their jobs. Most people agree that if a choice has to be made between caring and giving up paid employment, or remaining in employment and doing less caring, then the proper thing to do is to give priority to employment, although this need not imply that no support should be given to an elderly parent. It is therefore not surprising to find that the majority of carers in Britain combine caregiving with paid work (Arber and Ginn, 1995). In Canada in 2002, 70 per cent of caregivers aged 45 to 64 were employed (Pyper, 2006). What most employed caregivers seek in the decisions they make is not a stark choice between caring and employment, but some compromise which will enable them to do both. Women as well as men give priority to maintaining their employment position, making strenuous and sometimes ingenious efforts to do so as well as fulfilling such family responsibilities as they believe that they should acknowledge. Finding a compromise between caring and paid work that protects employment is seen as a highly desirable solution when people are faced with significant responsibilities towards kin.

Finch and Mason observed the following compromises in their research. First, the work of caring for an elderly parent may be shared, either between spouses or between siblings, so that the burden imposed on any one person is reduced. Second, leaves of absence from work may be used to cover times when there is a crisis and a temporary need for large amounts of care. Third, caregivers who have considerable autonomy in their job may be able to accommodate the caregiving into their work routine, as when someone whose job entails travelling is able to drop in on a relative as they go about their work. And fourth, caregivers may take on part-time work, which leaves them with sufficient free time in which to carry out their commitments to care. In these ways people are able to adjust their lives so that they can both care and remain in paid employment.

The majority of employed carers provide care for parents, other relatives and neighbours who are living in other households. There is little evidence that giving such care for under 20 hours per week reduces participation in paid employment. For the majority of carers, their caregiving role leads to work accommodation, such as reduced overtime or passing up an opportunity for a better job in a different locale, rather than influencing them to withdraw from the labour force entirely. However, the impacts on employment are not insignificant. We see this in a study of role conflict involving daughters who care for aged parents in Australia (Murphy *et al.*, 1997). Daughters reported the following ways in which caring affected their work. As a result of caregiving, daughters had less energy in their work, they had repeated interruptions at work, they altered work schedules to accommodate caring, they reduced their hours of employment, they took unpaid leave, and they refused promotions. A majority of employed daughters reported that caregiving had adversely affected their employment in one of these ways. The effects of caregiving upon employment, including withdrawal from work, were most notable where the care recipient lived with the daughter, the parent's disability was severe and, in turn, a greater intensity of care was provided.

Similar results emerge from a study in Canada (Pyper, 2006). In a survey conducted by Statistics Canada, respondents were asked if caregiving had caused them to reduce their hours of paid employment, change their work patterns, or turn down a job offer or promotion. They were also asked if caregiving had caused them to postpone education or training, or had led to a reduction in their income. The study found that caregivers providing relatively few hours of care per week were not affected very much. About three-quarters of women, and an even higher proportion of men, reported no job-related changes. On the other hand, those providing between one and four hours of care reported more job-related changes. And when higher degrees of caregiving and employment were combined, the job-related effects were greater still. Almost two-thirds of women and almost half of men who combined high levels of caregiving with paid employment had to make adjustments in their job.

In another study, Sara Arber and Jay Ginn have examined the relationship between paid employment and caregiving for women and men in Great Britain (Arber and Ginn, 1995). They found that the more hours women and men spend providing care each week, the lower is their level of employment participation. Where caring is provided in the home, the main significant effect is that men and women caring for more than 35 hours each week have much lower odds of being employed. This relationship is more pronounced for women than it is for men. Although most people who care do not give up paid employment, clearly some do, particularly if they are doing a lot of caring. Maria Evandrou and Karen Glaser report in another study from Britain that while the majority of men and women who care say that caring has no effect on their work arrangements, significant numbers do report such effects (Evandrou and Glaser, 2003). About one-fifth of mid-life women who had ever cared reported that they stopped work altogether, and another tenth reported that they worked fewer hours. Thus, nearly one-third of women who cared had reduced their labour market activity as a result of their caring, compared with under one-fifth of men. Although both men and women engage in caregiving, caring continues to be a gendered activity in Britain.

Evandrou and Glaser are especially concerned with the effects of caring upon lower lifetime earnings and upon lesser earnings-related benefits such as pensions. They report that a smaller proportion of men and women who stopped work as a result of caring were members of an occupational pension scheme compared with other groups. Among those who were members of such a plan, men and women who ceased working in order to provide care had accumulated fewer years of contributions than their counterparts who continued working. This has implications for quality of life in old age, as the value of pensions is partly related to the number of years in which contributions are made. Caregivers who give up their employment will have lower pension income in later life.

The effects of caregiving upon employment and related benefits vary according to the location where the care is provided. Co-resident caregivers are less likely to be employed than people giving care to someone living outside the household, among both women and men. This is partly because co-resident care is much more likely than extra-resident care to involve long hours of care each week. Arber and Ginn also hypothesize that this is because there is a stronger normative obligation to provide care for someone living in the same household than there is for someone living in a different household. Caring is more likely to affect employment participation when the caregiver has little choice about whether to provide care. That is most likely to apply in the case of co-resident care. Normative expectations in Britain are that women will take on the caregiving role for any household member who requires care. Men take on this role only when there is no female household member available to do so, such as when their spouse requires care. Such obligatory caregiving has a strong effect on employment participation.

The impact of obligatory caregiving varies by gender. There is a substantial gender difference in employment participation among those caring for a disabled child or elderly parent or parent-in-law in the home. For example, the effect on employment of caring for a co-resident parent or parent-in-law is least for married men and greatest for married women. In this situation, a married man's wife takes over the main responsibility for the caring role. Married men can rely on their wives to a considerable extent to perform caring roles, with the implication that it is the wife's employment rather than the husband's employment that is more likely to be adversely affected. It is only when there is no option, such as when their wife requires care, that married men's employment is severely affected. Unlike men, women have significantly lower odds of employment if they are providing co-resident care, irrespective of the kin relationship involved. Among men, there are significantly lower odds of employment associated with co-resident caregiving only when care is provided for a spouse.

A gender difference also exists for extra-resident care. Women are more likely than men to provide care for someone living in the same household or for someone living in a different household, but the gap is greatest for care given to someone living outside the household. Both sexes have obligations to provide co-resident care for a spouse, but the obligation to provide extra-resident care is stronger for women than it is for men. This is reflected in the different relationships between paid employment and caring for the two sexes. Among women, but not among men, caregiving is related to the distribution of employment between full-time and part-time work. Co-resident carers are less likely to work either full-time or part-time, but women who are extra-resident carers are only less likely to work full-time. Working part-time is in fact higher among women caring for someone who lives outside the home than it is either for women caring for someone living inside the home or for non-carers. Among men, there is no adverse effect of extra-resident caring on their employment. However, among women, providing extra-resident care is associated with a lower rate of full-time employment than among non-carers and a higher rate of part-time employment. It appears that providing extra-resident care does not induce most women to leave employment entirely, but it does lead many of them to substitute part-time employment for full-time employment. In this way many women are able to lessen the negative financial implications of time spent in caregiving, which would otherwise be considerable if employment were given up entirely. Giving up full-time employment in order to care is likely to have substantial negative consequences both for the carers' current financial position and for their old age through their inability to accumulate pension contributions.

Caregiving can have consequences for people's lives in addition to its possible consequences for employment. Under some conditions it can lead to a sense of caregiver burden, for example that the caregiver's health is affected, or that she or he does not have enough time for themselves. Caregiver burden is connected to the amount of caregiving provided, being higher among those who do more caring. Caring can lead to changes in social activities, changes to holiday plans, or extra expenses. These changes are more marked among people who spend more time on caregiving tasks than they are among people who spend less time in caring (Pyper, 2006). The socioeconomic effects of caregiving are also greater for women who are employed for longer periods of time. For example, Wendy Pyper reports from a Canadian study that among women providing four hours or more of caregiving per week, almost two-thirds of those who worked longer hours reported substantial consequences, compared with approximately half of those who were not employed (Pyper, 2006). Combining employment and caregiving results in a time crunch that affects people's non-working activities.

TENSIONS AROUND CARE

Women who provide care seem to resist giving up employment in order to do so. This may mean controlling the amount of care they give so that the total workload of paid employment and caregiving does not become too burdensome. Such a strategy can, however, create psychological tensions over how much care to provide, and it can lead to guilt feelings. In Canada, over two-fifths of women providing care report feelings of guilt, saying that they feel they should be doing more to help or that they should be doing a better job (Pyper, 2006). These feelings were especially strong among female caregivers who were involved in lower amounts of caregiving. In some cases this reduced level of caregiving is clearly due to a desire, or need, to accommodate paid employment. Not surprisingly, then, women working many hours a week were more likely to have guilt feelings. The highest incidence of guilt feelings was among women who worked longer hours and who provided relatively few hours of care. Here, seven out of ten women giving care reported having guilt feelings. Longer work hours may be preventing these women from doing as much caregiving as they would like, with the result that they feel bad about themselves. Male caregivers who work long hours and who provide lower levels of care are also likely to feel guilty, but not as much as women. Working longer hours was associated with increased guilt feelings among both men and women, but in general women were more likely than men to have feelings of guilt. Such feelings can be part of a broader set of tensions around care.

Jane Aronson has studied the tensions around care that daughters provide for elderly mothers in Toronto, Canada (Aronson, 1990). She reports that both mothers and daughters thought it was natural that a daughter should be the one to provide care to a dependent parent, but they both sought to limit the extent of this dependence. This limit-setting took the forms of: deliberately not sharing households with a mother or daughter; maintaining clear financial boundaries; limiting the amount of time devoted to assisting older mothers; and refusal by mothers to ask for or accept help under certain conditions. Setting limits to dependence in these ways created tensions for both mothers and daughters.

For daughters, tensions arose from a contradiction between feeling an obligation to provide care and not wanting to let the caregiving role take over their life. The position of daughters as carers is potentially very difficult. They must balance their responsibilities for parents with those for husbands and children, and the needs of their families with those of their employers. In Jane Aronson's study, daughters felt they should be doing more for their mothers by being more attentive to their needs and living up to an ideal of responsiveness and performance of duty. But then they also wanted to maintain all the other activities in their lives. This was a particularly strong feeling among women who were wives and mothers. They felt an obligation to look after their husbands and children first, and by comparison their commitments to their mothers were secondary. The competing demands of husbands and children for time and energy are believed to take priority over mothers' claims. (In England, Janet Finch and Jennifer Mason also report that it is believed the needs of the younger generation should take precedence over the needs of the older generation. Their research indicates that the claim to have prior commitments seems to be one of the most important procedural rules which comes into play in deciding who should take responsibility for an aged parent.) Filial obligations clearly have limits that are set by the need to fulfil other responsibilities which are seen as having a higher priority.

At the same time, daughters who do not provide what they believe is an appropriate level of care for their mothers may feel guilty about their failure to do so. This is particularly likely among women who hold a highly idealized image of family life, which is impossible to realize in practice.

For mothers, tension arose from a contradiction between recognizing a need for care and at the same time not wanting to become too dependent upon their daughters. They experienced or anticipated a need for support, but they felt that they should let their daughters get on with their own lives and not overburden them. Elderly mothers felt ambivalent about the fact they were unable to look after themselves unaided when they also wanted to be self-reliant and undemanding. They strove to balance a wish for support and security with a wish to behave in accordance with norms of self-reliance and individualism. These older women shared the younger women's assumptions about their relatively low priority in family life, and they did not want to be too demanding. If they were dissatisfied with their daughters' lack of attention, they felt ashamed of wanting more from their daughters than they believed their daughters should be delivering.

The caring relationship between daughters and their mothers can be difficult, and pose problems for both parties. It can give rise to ambivalent feelings in which the individual feels torn between different impulses. Jane Lewis and Barbara Meredith have explored this issue for daughters who have cared for elderly mothers in Britain (Lewis and Meredith, 1988). They report that women who care for an elderly parent have a deep desire to do so, for reasons of affection, obligation, reciprocity and just the feeling that it is natural for daughters to do so. Caring may be a part of their identity, so that the question of whether not to care never arises. Daughters can feel a profound loyalty to their mothers, and want to protect them from the intrusions of strangers. Allied to this is the feeling that many daughters know what is best for their mothers. Positive feelings about caring can be derived from the companionship, emotional security, sense of being needed, and appreciation that it brings to the carer, especially in cases where the caring relationship is successful and supported by recognition from others about the importance of their contributions. At the same time they often have negative feelings about the impact that caring has upon their lives.

Daughters who have cared for elderly mothers may feel bitter about the financial costs of providing care, feeling that the lack of financial reward for their role is the concrete manifestation of a general lack of recognition for what they do. This can occur, for instance, if their career progress has suffered from their lack of flexibility and mobility. Missed opportunities may continue to bother them long after the caregiving period is over. Such feelings are particularly likely if women have to give up working in order to care, or reduce their employment to part-time work, because to the financial loss is added a loss of outside interests and identity. In Australia, Barbara Murphy and her colleagues report that there appears to be inherent fulfilment and satisfaction in maintaining roles other than that of carer. Carers with partners, those with children, and those in paid jobs were generally happier with their lives. Working women commonly found their work a source of respite from caregiving, and an opportunity to take up other interests. Not surprisingly, daughters who had quit work in order to care for an elderly parent reported higher resentment than all other groups (Murphy *et al.*, 1997).

Daughters may also experience their mothers as too demanding, and wish that they could do more for themselves. Also, they may feel a lack of purpose at the end of the caregiving period, when the elderly parent dies or has to be institutionalized, because now they have to put their lives back together and decide what they want to do with the sudden increase in available time. They may have made no plans for their own lives, leading perhaps to increased anxieties about their own old age. Allowing a mother to go into institutional care can also bring on feelings of guilt that the daughter has not lived up to her commitments to her mother.

Daughters who have cared for elderly mothers can have feelings of resentment about what they believe is an inappropriate level of support from other family members, friends or government service providers. This becomes a special issue when the elderly parent becomes more disabled, and a heavier burden of care falls upon the primary caregiver. As the intensity of the caring relationship increases with advanced disability, access to the help which can be a buffer against stress may become more difficult. Neighbours and friends, who may have dropped by earlier to provide assistance, tend to withdraw as the caring tasks become more demanding, and perhaps distasteful. Friends (of both the person cared for and the carer), for example, may no longer offer help when it becomes a matter of dealing with incontinence or senile dementia. Caregivers may also find formal services unpredictable and unreliable, and therefore unsatisfactory. However, even when neither mother nor daughter is well supported by kin, friends or professionals, the daughters are still likely to have positive feelings about caring if the social relationship between mother and daughter has always been good and remains so. The most important factor determining how the carer feels about caring appears to be the quality of the caring relationship. Where the social relationship is problematic, and the carer can expect no positive appreciation from her mother, then caregiving is likely to be experienced as more difficult.

THE CONTRIBUTION OF ELDERLY PEOPLE

Daughters in particular, and children in general, are not the only ones who provide care for elderly people. The elderly also are providers of care to elderly people. The largest contribution to caregiving in Britain is made by women in their early 60s (Arber and Ginn, 1990). Older people are givers as well as receivers, when, for example, they care for grand-children. The most notable care provided by older people, however, is care for each other, particularly care between spouses. When one spouse becomes infirm and unable to look after themselves, it is usually their partner who is the first person to provide assistance. This reflects the strong norm of mutual support between spouses who live together. In Britain, the majority of carers are spouses (Lewis and Meredith, 1988). The average amount of time spent providing such care increases dramat-ically with age. Among co-resident carers, substantially more time is spent caring for dependants as the carer's age increases. Even in the oldest age groups the bulk of co-resident carers are spouses. Interest-ingly, there is no difference in the proportion of wives and husbands who care for their elderly spouse. Among the elderly there is gender equality in providing co-resident care, though elderly women provide more care for people outside the household. Men provide a significant proportion of the total volume of informal care for elderly people, which is generally overlooked. The attention paid to daughters caring for their parents and parents-in-law needs to be complemented by recognizing the substantial volume of care provided by elderly spouses, both husbands and wives.

The dominant view of the elderly in social policy discourse is that they constitute a social problem in which the burden of their care falls on other age groups. This negative view of the elderly neglects the amount of care that the elderly provide for each other. In Britain, over one-third of the informal care provided for elderly people is provided by the elderly themselves (Arber and Ginn, 1990). Taking the care provided by elderly people into account might lead to social policies that help the elderly to become better caregivers.

DISCUSSION

Caregiving is a challenging task which frequently becomes more demand-ing as the care recipient ages and the level of frailty increases. Under such conditions tensions may arise as the elderly recipients of care regret their declining autonomy, and care providers regret the impact of caregiving upon the rest of their life. The latter tensions become especially acute when caregivers have to give up paid employment in order to care. Whether such situations lead to resentment or not depends heavily upon the quality of the social relationship between caregiver and care recipient, which depends in turn upon the quality of the relationship that they have enjoyed in the past. When there is considerable resentment, the relationship between caregiver and care recipient may deteriorate to the point where it involves violence or exploitation directed at the care recipient. This is a general problem that requires more attention.

8 Violence and sexual abuse

Violence and sexual abuse, mainly by men against women and children, have received increased attention in recent years (Wood and Jewkes, 1997). Once a hidden subject, it has been brought into the open and subjected to public scrutiny and academic research. This has meant revealing the inner lives of families. Much violence and sexual abuse of women and children occurs within the family. For example, women are most at risk of murder inside their own homes. Most female homicide victims die at the hands of their male partners, usually after a history of domestic violence. Contrary to prevailing stereotypes, most victims of rape are not raped by total strangers. The majority of rapes and other forms of sexual abuse are committed by someone the victim knows, including people to whom they are related (Shalhoub-Kevorkian, 1999).

One hidden dimension of violence and sexual abuse towards females has been the case of marital rape (Gelles, 1977). Wives do not always want to have sex with their husbands, perhaps because the husbands have come home drunk or at odd hours. Husbands, on the other hand, tend to believe that their wives should have intercourse with them on demand. Some husbands view a refusal of intercourse as grounds for beating or intimidating their wives.

The fact that a number of women are forced into having sexual relations with their husbands as a result of intimidation or physical force was neglected until recently. Women who were forced into having sexual intercourse with their husbands were thought to 'ask for', 'deserve' or 'enjoy' their victimization. Largely as a result of the impact of the feminist movement, this perception has begun to change. The feminist movement has brought problems previously considered personal to public attention. It has also engaged in critical scrutiny of the family, which feminists have identified as an important structure of domination (Breines and Gordon, 1983). Until feminist scholarship demystified it, the family was accepted by most scholars as an harmonious institution which was the site of love and intimacy. It can be those things, but it is also the site of power and violence. Feminist studies stress the importance of analysing the family as a locus of struggle and conflict as well as of support. This analysis points to gender and age structuring as a source of power differences and personal tensions. Individuals acquire different degrees of power depending upon their sex, class, race and age. People often hurt one another in patterns that reflect the power, or lack of it, that different family members hold in society. These differences are acted out in intimate relationships. The family is therefore seen as an institution that permits, and sometimes encourages, its members to hurt one another physically or psychologically.

In the family, violence and hate are felt, expressed and learned as consistently as love. For example, there are more murder victims who are members of the murderer's family than any other category of murderer–victim relationship, and people are more likely to observe, commit or be a victim of violence within their family than in any other setting. Included in this changed perception of family life is an assumption that rape may be more an act of power in the relation between a man and a woman than an act of passion gone wrong. Marital rape must be seen in the context of wider power relations, and, in principle, it may not be fundamentally different from other means of exerting power over another person. It is seen as being produced within a gendered society in which male power predominates. Men tend to have more power than women, and rape may be an expression of that power. Both sex and violence are means that husbands can use to dominate and control their wives.

FORCED MARRIAGE

Forced sex within marriage is only part of the oppression exercised against women and female children. Another aspect is forced marriage, which is found in some countries and communities. In parts of West Africa, for example, girls as young as ten are forced into marriages mandated by their parents (Ouattara, Sen and Thomson, 1998). Some girls are betrothed by their parents at or even before birth. This bond may be a result of friendship ties, or based on a system of exchanging women between groups. The future husband may give presents to his future in-laws or provide services for them in recognition of the benefits of the wife-to-be. As a result, parents feel a strong obligation to respect the pledge they have made, and they force the girl to marry the man they have chosen even if that is against her wishes. In Nepal, also, arranged marriages are common in which girls are forced to marry the husbands chosen for them. Reasons for arranging marriage include the fact that the girls are needed to provide domestic help for the boy's family, grandparents desire to see their granddaughter settled before they die, and parents believe that marriage of girls before menstruation is holy. Also, parents may direct their children into early marriage with an appropriate boy because they fear their daughter may develop an inappropriate relationship with a boy from another caste, or because they fear their daughter eloping with someone who is otherwise judged to be unsuitable.

The negative effects of forced early marriage include interrupted schooling resulting in lower education, overloading of domestic and family responsibilities, lack of outside social activities including inability to maintain friendship ties and health risks associated with early pregnancy and childbearing. Young mothers are also often ill-prepared for motherhood and have a higher incidence of infant mortality. Child brides are also more vulnerable to sexual abuse in marriage including marital rape. In a study of marriage in India, Purna Sen found that brides who had been married at or below the age of 15 had one of the highest rates of vulnerability to sexual violence in marriage (Ouattara, Sen and Thomson, 1998). This includes sexual intercourse before the onset of menstruation, early and very painful sex and forced sexual activity with their husbands even when they had indicated an unwillingness to do so. Under such conditions there is no possibility for girls to give or withhold personal permission for sexual activity. Forced early marriage gives a man licence to impose sex upon a girl, denying her control over her own body including whether, when, and with whom she has sexual relations. In the vast majority of cases, communities are unwilling to confront the rape of young girls which goes on in the name of marriage. As a result, the rape of young girls is supported by the social legitimacy of marriage.

CHILD MORTALITY

Forced marriage and forced sex are not the only risks faced by children in families. Another is premature death. This is more of a problem in some countries than in others, particularly where there is gender inequality in child mortality rates. In China, for example, there is higher female mortality than male mortality during early childhood (Choe, Hongsheng and Feng, 1995). This is contrary to the usual pattern of higher male mortality than female mortality. The pattern of higher female child mortality appears to be related to a local cultural preference for sons. This follows from the traditional family system in China being based upon patrilineal and patriarchal principles. Son preference has persisted despite the communist revolution, modernization and industrialization. This preference is evident in fertility behaviour, and it appears that it may also affect parental behaviour in caring for young children, which in turn produces differential mortality rates.

The Chinese cultural preference for sons seems to result in young girls receiving less parental care and attention than young boys. Girls are therefore more likely to die from the early childhood diseases of respiratory infections, other infections and parasitic diseases, diarrhoeal diseases and accidents. Higher female child mortality indicates that there is unequal treatment of female and male children within the family in such behaviours as obtaining immunization, quality of care during illness, exposure to risks and allocation of resources including food.

Preference for sons is not evident from mortality statistics on first-born children in China (Choe, Hongsheng and Feng, 1995). It appears that Chinese parents value a first girl child as much as they value a first boy child. This may be because first-born female children are seen as contributing to the family economy through performing household duties and also contributing to household income through their employment. Among subsequent children, however, the data on differential mortality suggest that girls are not valued as highly as boys. It is especially note-worthy that in families which have older girls only, subsequent female children are at a much higher risk of childhood mortality than are subsequent male children. Among female children in families with more than one child, girls who have only brothers experience the least mortality disadvantage. Discrimination against female children in China seems to start with second daughters.

Higher female mortality in childhood has been found in countries other than China, especially in populations where there is a strong cultural preference for sons such as those in South Asia. India is a country with a pervasive preference for sons, and it has one of the highest levels of excess child mortality for girls (Arnold, Choe and Roy, 1998). However, the strength of son preference varies from one part of the country to another, and excess female child mortality is higher in the North of India than it is in the South. Like China, girls with older sisters are often subject to the highest risks of mortality.

Son preference in India has deep economic, social and religious roots. In rural areas, sons are valued because of the assistance they can provide in agricultural production, and more generally sons are important for their contributions to the economic security of their parents in old age. Sons bring higher status to the family, and they bring economic resources in the form of dowry payments. Finally, sons are important for their role in religious performances, such as lighting the funeral pyre for the cremation of deceased parents. Daughters, on the other hand, have low status, and they are seen as an economic liability because of the necessity to make dowry payments for them as well as the high cost of weddings. Daughters also have a weaker relationship with the natal family, because when they marry they go to live with their husband's family and have more contact with them.

Son preference is thought to be the principal cause of excess female child mortality in India. Parents who prefer sons to daughters provide inferior care to daughters in terms of food allocation, prevention of diseases and accidents, and treatment when the child is sick. For example, boys have a consistent advantage over girls in immunization against the major childhood diseases, especially in states with a strong son preference. Also, when girls become ill they are less likely than boys to receive medical treatment.

DOWRY-RELATED VIOLENCE

As noted above, one of the factors associated with son preference in India is the dowry system. The dowry system can also have other disadvantages for women. One of these disadvantages is violence against married women by their husbands and other members of the husband's family, as a result of the failure of the woman's parents to make substantial dowry payments (Prasad, 1994). Married women are emotionally and physically abused, murdered or driven to commit suicide because of persistent demands for dowry. Beating, torturing by administering electric shocks, branding, disfiguring, keeping the woman confined without food and threatening desertion have all been reported as abuses perpetrated by the bride's spouse and her in-laws. Dowry issues are a significant cause of the murders of women in India, and burning women alive after pouring kerosene on them is a common cause of death in dowry murders. (Kerosene is commonly used in cooking in India and it is therefore readily available in kitchens. Its use in murders of women is possibly intended as a means of trying to disguise a murder as an accident or suicide.)

In India, a woman's value to her husband and in-laws is enhanced when she is accompanied by a substantial dowry. Dowry is seen by many young men and their families as a legitimate means of clearing family debts, acquiring luxury goods and improving social standing. Increasingly, dowry takes the form of money payments and consumer items rather than goods related to the wife's domestic role. As a result, married women have less control over their dowry, and a mercenary attitude has been encouraged that stresses the financial benefit to the husband and his family. The fact that married women have less control over cash and consumer items reinforces the dependent status of the woman and makes her more vulnerable to abuse.

Dowry in India is not a one-time payment, but it consists of an open-ended commitment to make payments both at the time of the marriage and subsequently. Therefore, the opportunity exists to put pressure on the wife's natal family to make generous payments after the marriage has taken place. An amount of dowry may be agreed upon and paid, but later comes to be seen as insufficient leading to new demands. Behind these demands there is often the unspoken threat of abuse of the bride after marriage. Wife-giving families that do not meet the demands made upon them may have to face the frustration and anger of the wife-taker's family. This may eventually contribute to abuse of the bride by her husband and her in-laws.

People who may assault the bride include, in addition to the husband, the mother-in-law, siblings of the husband and occasionally other members of the family. In one study of dowry-related violence reported in the newspapers, husbands were most often mentioned as the abusers, followed by their mothers, their brothers, their sisters and lastly by other relatives (Prasad, 1994). Dowry victimization occurs most often when the woman is living in an extended or joint household. That is because in such contexts the wife's in-laws join her husband in perpetrating the abuse.

WIFE BEATING

Violence towards wives is not random, but it occurs in a cultural context of beliefs that define women as inferior and subject to the will of their husbands. Failure to follow the wishes of their husbands therefore becomes grounds for inflicting harm upon them. Forms of violence towards wives such as wife beating therefore tend to be found in contexts where there is a strong patriarchal ideology which justifies male control over females.

One society in which patriarchal ideology is strongly entrenched is that of Palestine. Here, the husband is culturally accepted as the ruler of the family, and he is regarded as the ultimate authority whom the wife and children must obey. Women are seen as being placed under male control to safeguard them and to ensure that they follow appropriate moral standards. A husband is expected to protect the reputation of his family, and he assumes the responsibility for maintaining the family structure by whatever means he feels are justified.

Muhammad Haj-Yahia has studied this ideology and its implications for violence towards wives among Palestinian men (Haj-Yahia, 1998). He found that beliefs justifying wife beating were most common among men with traditional and patriarchal attitudes towards women, traditional and patriarchal expectations of marital roles and patriarchal beliefs about the family. The strongest approval of wife beating was expressed with regard to the belief that a sexually unfaithful wife deserves to be beaten, with lesser agreement to wife beating if she insulted him in front of his friends or challenged his manhood. Similarly, Palestinian men were most likely to blame battered wives as having caused the violence against them if they had patriarchal and non-egalitarian expectations of marriage, they had patriarchal beliefs about the family, and they held conservative beliefs about sexuality. This included the belief that a wife would not be beaten if she knew her boundaries and how to avoid her husband, and the belief that a battered wife must have done something to irritate her husband.

DISCUSSION

Violence and sexual abuse in the family, especially against women and children, are world-wide problems. Everywhere they are related to power differentials in relationships, and especially to the social subordination of women. Wife beating and marital rape, for example, are instances in which more powerful males inflict harm upon weaker females. These patterns of behaviour are legitimated and protected by patriarchal ideologies that define the family as an arena in which men have higher status than women, and in which the demands of men receive greater recognition than the desires of women. The solution to this problem is to give women and children greater control over their lives. This includes the right not to be forced into marriage at an early age. Family formation should be a voluntary act, not something that is imposed by more powerful individuals.

9 Family formation

Families are formed in various ways. Traditionally, the principal mode of family formation in most societies has been through legal marriage. A couple decide (or are promised by their parents) to live together indefinitely, and they cement their bond by seeking community approval for the match in the form of a public marriage ceremony. In every society, there is some expectation of the normal age at which marriage will occur. However, the average age of marriage varies from one society to another, and it has varied over time. In many societies the trend in recent decades has been for the average of marriage to increase. People are getting married at older ages, which normally means that they also begin having children at older ages as well. Older age at marriage is often associated with smaller completed family size, as women who marry young have more children. Women who marry young tend to picture their ideal family as relatively large, they are less likely to take active steps to limit fertility, and they have more children. Those who marry after age 20 have a faster pace of childbearing following marriage, but completed fertility is higher among those who marry before age 20 because the latter have a longer period of exposure to the risk of childbearing (Heaton, 1996). That is because, among most peoples, it is expected that a couple will not begin childbearing until they are married, and marriage therefore publically legitimates the couple's right to have children.

Marriage is not the only mode of family formation, however. A couple may just decide to start living together, and this has become increasingly common in a number of Western societies in recent decades. Cohabitation is now an established practice in many places, and predictions are that the upward trend will continue. As a result, the beginning of cohabitation may be a more apt marker of family formation than date of marriage. Cohabitation is sometimes a permanent state that rivals marriage as a means of family formation, but in other cases cohabitation is followed by marriage after a period of time, as the couple seek public recognition for their private arrangement. The decision to marry seems to be most likely at the point in their relationship when the couple decide that they want to have children together.

Childbearing does not always follow marriage, of course, and sometimes families are formed when women have children without being married or even without living with a man. Sometimes this childbearing outside marriage or cohabitation is involuntary, being due to accidental pregnancy, especially among adolescents. On other occasions, childbearing outside marriage or cohabitation is the result of a woman's voluntary choice to raise children on her own. This pattern of behaviour seems to have become increasingly more common in some societies in recent years, as women have gained greater autonomy and control over their lives. Increased non-marital childbearing has been attributed to greater economic independence of women made possible by higher rates of labour force activity, rising wages of younger, more educated cohorts, and the availability of means-tested income support programmes for poor, single mothers. In particular, when women have their own sources of income, they have little financial incentive to marry men with poor market prospects. Jobless men, and those with highly unstable employment histories, are less attractive as marriage partners because they are not reliable family providers. However, despite all the changes that have occurred, marriage usually remains the most popular means of family formation.

AGE AT MARRIAGE

Marriage usually implies for women the assumption of greater domestic responsibilities and, after varying periods of time, the commencement of childbearing. That is because the traditional role for married women has emphasized their responsibilities as housewives and mothers. Marriage therefore has a large impact on women's lives and it is an important event in their life course. Recent changes in marriage have therefore been changing women's lives. A substantial social science literature has shown that changes in female education and labour force participation in the process of modernization translate into new roles and aspirations for women that often conflict with the traditional roles of wife and mother. Lower ages at marriage are associated with rural societies, low levels of education for both men and women, and low rates of female labour force participation before and after marriage. On the other hand, the strongest and most consistent predictors of later age at marriage are women's education and their employment in non-agricultural activities. As a result of increases in female education and employment that occur with modernization, age at marriage for women has increased and the proportion of women remaining single has grown.

The effect of marriage on women varies according to the age at which marriage takes place. Delays in the timing of first union are relevant because they reduce the amount of time women are exposed to the risk of conception, and therefore fertility, and because they increase the availability of alternative social roles for women. For example, later age at marriage is usually associated with later school leaving and there- fore with more education than that received by women who marry at younger ages. One of the changes that has been occurring in women's lives lately is a trend towards increased age at marriage, which is correlated with their increased education.

Analysis of the relationship between age at marriage and education is complicated by the fact that the direction of causation can run both ways. On one hand, age at marriage can influence educational attain- ment because females usually discontinue education before marriage. On the other hand, women with higher educational aspirations may delay marriage. In Venezuela, for example, being enrolled in school signifi- cantly reduces the risk of entering a union, whether legal or consensual (Parrado and Tienda, 1997). Controlling for other variables, Venezuelan women who are enrolled in school are half as likely to enter a union than women who are not attending school. Increased school enrolment is therefore the main factor behind the observed delay in the timing of first unions for Venezuelan women. In Germany also, women have been increasing their educational attainments and their subsequent occupational opportunities, with implications for marriage. Hans-Peter Blossfeld and Johannes Huinink report from a detailed empirical study that this shift is associated with increasing age of marriage (Blossfeld and Huinink, 1991). Educational expansion has a delaying effect on the timing of first marriage, they claim, as attending school, vocational train- ing programmes or a university has a strong negative effect on the rate of entry into marriage. Blossfeld and Huinink hypothesize that marriage is postponed because women delay the transition from youth to adulthood while they are receiving their education. Participation in education takes time and it affects women's ability to marry. That is partly because women who attend school do not have the time to perform the roles of housewives and mothers, and they therefore postpone marriage so that they can complete their education. Also, there are normative expectations in German society that young people who are participating in the educational system should not marry. That is because it is the conventional belief that the familial roles of wife and mother create time constraints which may interfere with continuation of schooling, and in today's world most parents want their daughters to get a good education. Finishing one's education therefore counts as one of the important prerequisites for entering into marriage.

Tim Heaton has explored the relationship between education and age at marriage in three Islamic societies: Egypt, Jordan and Indonesia (Heaton, 1996). These are societies in which women have traditionally tended to marry at young ages. In all three societies, there has been a substantial increase in age at marriage, with notable declines in the proportion of women marrying before age 20. This trend is related to changing educational experiences. Well over half of women with no schooling are married by age 20 in each country, compared with fewer than 10 per cent of those with post-secondary education. Heaton concludes that education thus plays a major role in delaying marriage. Women who complete more schooling wait longer to marry. The positive relationship between education and age at marriage, and the sharp decline in early marriage observed in recent cohorts, indicate that important changes are under way in the Islamic world. Muslim women are spending more years in late adolescence unmarried, and this is important because a rise in age at marriage generally translates into lower fertility.

As we have seen, education is one alternative to marriage that is available to modern women. Another alternative is employment outside the home in the market economy, which decreases the need for economic dependence upon a man. As alternatives to marriage open up for modern women, marriage may become less attractive compared with other opportunities, and women may delay or even reject marriage. From a macro-sociological perspective, later age at marriage for women may therefore be related to societal modernization. With modernization, a wider range of socioeconomic opportunities become available, and marriage ceases to be the only viable opportunity for economic and social well-being. In less developed societies, women are often economically dependent upon men, and marriage to a man is therefore essential for adult survival. In more developed societies, however, women can often earn enough or receive enough in state benefits to support themselves and their children without the aid of a man. In such societies, education is one important avenue to better employment prospects, and obtaining a good education becomes an important life goal. This in turn decreases the attractiveness of early marriage.

Fakhrul Chowdhury and Frank Trovato have examined the modernization hypothesis of age at marriage for five Asian societies at different levels of development (Chowdhury and Trovato, 1994). These societies are Bangladesh, Pakistan, Nepal, Sri Lanka and Malaysia. Of these societies, Sri Lanka and Malaysia are the most developed, having, for example, a higher percentage of the working population employed in the non-agricultural sector and higher levels of female literacy. These two countries also have higher mean ages at marriage for women.

In all five countries, women with higher levels of education have an older age at marriage. Age at marriage is also related to whether women are involved in no work, or in agricultural activities, or in non-agricultural activities. A later age at marriage is found for women who were employed in the market economy. Also, women employed in professional, administrative, skilled and other white collar jobs have a higher age at marriage than the national average. These differences are wider in Sri Lanka and Malaysia than they are in the other three countries. In all countries the average age at marriage for women engaged in professional jobs is higher than for other occupational groups. Presumably this is partly because professional women postpone marriage for an extended period while they complete their education, and partly because of their occupational aspirations to establish themselves in their careers before getting married.

COHABITATION

Large increases in the proportion of young persons who are not married is commonly interpreted to mean that young people are staying single longer. However, being unmarried is not synonymous with being single in every country, as couples may cohabit without getting married. In Western societies, delayed age at marriage does not necessarily mean delayed age of living together since premarital cohabitation has become increasingly common. Normative pressures towards marriage appear to have become very weak, but the attractions of living together are still relatively strong. Young people often set up home with partners of the opposite sex at almost as early an age as they did before marriage rates began to decline. As a result, in the United States, for example, the percentage of those who were ever in a union before age 20 has declined at a slower rate than the percentage ever married before age 20 (Bumpass, Sweet and Cherlin, 1991).

In some countries in the developing world, cohabitation has traditionally been quite prevalent. For example, in the Caribbean and Central America consensual unions have been a historical characteristic of the region. These informal unions therefore differ from the cohabitation found in more developed societies. In Venezuela, for example, consensual unions are consistently more prevalent among young women of rural origin and with low levels of education (Parrado and Tienda, 1997). The main factor behind cohabitation here appears to be low socioeconomic status. Cohabitation is a less desirable status than marriage, but not all women are able to achieve it. It is a constraint imposed on women with low socioeconomic status because of their poverty and because of their low bargaining power relative to men. In contrast to this traditional pattern of cohabitation, a more modern pattern of cohabitation has emerged in recent years among more educated women. For young women, higher levels of education increase the likelihood of cohabiting relative to the pattern for more mature women. This result is consistent with the proposition that, among younger women, consensual unions constitute an alternative choice for women with higher levels of education. Increased cohabitation among younger Venezuelans seems to be the result of an increased tendency for more educated women to choose cohabitation as their first type of union. This modern form of cohabitation is the result of a choice made by women who have various opportunities open to them to engage in a trial period of living together before marriage or to cohabit as a preferred alternative to marriage.

Marriage and cohabitation are alternatives between which people may choose. Cohabitation is very much a family status, as many cohabitors have children, for example. However, it is a status in which levels of certainty about the relationship are lower than in marriage. It is therefore possible to ask what are the characteristics of those who choose to cohabit compared with those who marry. For one thing, Bumpass and colleagues report for the United States that cohabiting couples express concern that getting married would place constraints on their personal freedom (Bumpass, Sweet and Cherlin, 1991). They note that men seem much more concerned about the effect of marriage on their independence than women.

In Australia, Helen Glezer has conducted a study about some of the antecedents of cohabitation (Glezer, 1993). In particular, she examined the family background and early adult experiences that influence or are associated with premarital cohabitation. Her findings reveal that people who cohabit tend to be relatively young, from urban rather than rural areas, and non-religious. People who cohabited compared with those who did not cohabit prior to first marriage tended to have liberal family values, and also valued marriage and children less than those who had not cohabited. They also had higher levels of individualism, stressing personal autonomy, than those who did not cohabit. Not surprisingly, individuals who cohabited also tended to have left home early and to have had early sexual relations. Glezer also found that women who cohabited were more likely to have grown up in families where parents were permissive and placed no restrictions on young adults leaving home or engaging in premarital sexual relations. On the other hand, women from families that discouraged leaving home and prohibited premarital sexual behaviour were less likely to cohabit. No such pattern was found for men. Among both men and women, individuals who were unhappy living with their family, or who did not feel accepted by their parents and felt there was a high level of tension in the home, were found to be far more likely to leave home early and to cohabit than individuals who reported a happy family upbringing.

Cohabitation can be an unstable state, in which couples either split up or get married. For example, in Great Britain most cohabiting unions last only a short time before dissolving or being converted into marriage (Ermisch and Francesconi, 1998). The decision by cohabiting couples to get married is sometimes related to a prior decision to begin having children. Traditionally, couples got married and then had a child. However, in Western societies the link between marriage and child-birth has become more complex in recent decades. Couples may cohabit and then when they wish to have children they may choose to marry before the woman gets pregnant. Some cohabiting couples wait until the woman gets pregnant before marrying. In Germany, for example, cohabiting women become much more likely to get married if they become pregnant (Blossfeld *et al.*, 1999). Normative pressure to marry may be weak, but there still seems to be a great desire among young Germans to avoid illegitimate births and to legalize the union before a child is born. Pregnancy can also lead to the breakdown of a consensual union if there is a strong disagreement over the desirability of having a child. And some women who are neither married nor cohabiting may decide to have children on their own.

CHILDBEARING

Union formation and birth are alternative pathways to family formation. In the latter case, new families are formed when single, unattached women give birth to children. In countries such as the United States, non-marital childbearing has become more prominent over the past several decades as rates of marital childbearing have declined and rates of non-marital childbearing have held steady or increased (Furstenberg, 1994). Some-times the incidence of families formed in this way is related to socio-economic characteristics such as race. In the United States, for example, births to single mothers occur at twice the rate for non-white women as for white women. The rate of premarital childbirth among Blacks is especially high, and it has been attributed in part to Blacks' lower marriage rates. Out-of-wedlock childbearing has become a far more important source of single parenthood for all Americans, but especially so for African-Americans who now have a sizable majority of first births before marriage. In particular, there is a much higher incidence of teen parenting among black inner-city residents.

Persisting racial differences in propensities to marry and to bear children out of wedlock, and the changing economic experiences of different racial groups, have rekindled debates about the relative importance of cultural factors versus economic factors in the causation of childbearing by single mothers. In particular, it is noteworthy that single mothers who belong to racial minorities are more likely than white mothers to have been reared in poverty. It is therefore difficult to disentangle the effects on family formation of minority status compared with low income. Haya Stier and Marta Tienda have examined this question in a study of inner-city neighbourhoods in Chicago (Stier and Tienda, 1997).

Stier and Tienda found that pathways to family formation are related to both economic conditions and race. Among non-African-American mothers, poverty appears to be the decisive factor that influences the likelihood of forming a family via birth. Poor women are less inclined to marry, and they are therefore more likely to enter into family life by giving birth. For example, family formation patterns of white urban women differed greatly depending on family income and neighbourhood poverty status. Approximately one-third of white women who either had low family income or who lived in low-income neighbourhoods formed families through a birth, compared with about one eighth of white mothers nationally. But among all low-income mothers, the share who entered family life through births was much greater among African-Americans than it was among Whites or Hispanics. Whereas approximately one-third of low-income white and Hispanic urban mothers formed families via birth, nearly four-fifths of urban poor African-American mothers did so. These results suggest a race effect on family formation in addition to a poverty effect. Stier and Tienda conclude that differences in family formation patterns by race cannot be reduced to differences in poverty status, although poverty is a factor.

In order to explore the meanings that low-income African-American mothers give to their lives, Linda Blum and Theresa Deussen interviewed 20 such mothers, most of whom were unmarried (Blum and Deussen, 1996). These women did not see marriage as an essential feature of family life, although in most cases they valued maintaining relationships with their children's fathers. Instead, they emphasized their independence and the capacity of strong women to manage on their own. In many cases they had role models in their mothers who had brought them up without being married. Their independence did not mean that these women were without assistance, as they relied on kin, particularly their sisters and mothers, for help in raising their children. These African-American women followed a pattern of community-based independence, based on non-marital relationships with male partners and shared care of children.

Although the incidence of family formation via birth is higher among African-American women than it is among white women, the former are not the only ones to enter into family life by giving birth. On the contrary, the incidence of premarital births has also been increasing among white women in recent years. Similarly, low-income women are not the only economic group to form families through birth. The prevalence of births outside marriage has also been increasing among middle-class women. In this context, Jane Bock has explored the meanings that single mothers by choice give to their decisions to bear children on their own, in a study of middle-class, mid-life, suburban white women in Southern California (Bock, 2000). These women believed that they were good mothers, and they justified entering into solo motherhood on the grounds that they possessed the essential attributes for motherhood. Increasingly, white middle-class single mothers argue that they are competent parents who are well qualified to mother on their own.

The women studied by Jane Bock did not challenge the normative order which sees marriage followed by motherhood as the normal course of events. They claimed that they supported the institution of marriage and that they would like to be in committed relationships, but that they had difficulty finding men who wanted to trade individualism for commitment. They had entered into single motherhood only after having given the matter much thought, and after they were sure that they possessed the attributes which they saw as entitling certain women to pursue single parenthood. Four primary attributes of entitlement were identified by them: age, responsibility, emotional maturity, and fiscal capability.

According to Bock's respondents, age is one of the most prominent attributes qualifying someone for single parenthood. Single women in mid-life face the prospect that they cannot wait much longer before having a child. At the same time, they began to re-evaluate the focus of their lives at mid-life and they realized that they needed new dimensions and relationships in their lives. They came to believe that motherhood could provide an important means of enriching their lives that a job could not. Bearing or adopting a child in mid-life also meant that single mothers by choice had allowed sufficient time for the normative pattern of marriage to occur. When it did not, their age also meant that they had been working long enough to have established themselves in careers that gave them financial security. Single mothers by choice also believed that they were entitled to enter into parenthood because they possessed the necessary personal qualities to take on the great responsibility of motherhood. They believed that they were responsible persons who were competent to make all the decisions about raising a child on their own. A related factor stressed by these women was their emotional maturity. They saw themselves as self-confident people who could manage emotionally on their own, and who possessed the necessary patience to raise a child. Finally, the women saw themselves as being sufficiently financially secure to be able to manage parenthood without the benefit of a man's income. Having spent time focused on their careers, they were at a point in their lives where they had good incomes. Their financial capacity meant that they were able to provide all of the things that a child needs. This, in their eyes, was the primary factor legitimizing their decision to parent alone. These middle-class single mothers by choice therefore saw themselves as being different from low-income single parents and therefore as entitled to respect from the community. They did not want to be viewed as problematic single parents, and they felt that their economic situation was sufficient to legitimize their decision to become mothers. By possessing all of these attributes (i.e. being sufficiently old, responsible, emotionally mature, and financially stable), these single women who chose motherhood were able to provide justifications to support their non-traditional route to beginning a family.

DISCUSSION

In this chapter we have seen that families can be formed in three ways. They can begin when a couple get married, or when they start living together, or when a single woman who is neither married nor cohabiting has a child. In countries like the United States, marriage has been declining as a basis for family formation. The number of cohabiting couples has increased, and more women are bearing children on their own. Nevertheless, marriage remains the most popular mode of family formation in the majority of places, and many families which begin with the couple moving in together are later legitimized through marriage. Marriage, too, has been changing. In most parts of the world, the frequency of marriages arranged entirely by the parents has declined, although parents still often play an important role in the selection of marriage partners (Kendall, 1996). Also, the average age at marriage has been increasing, especially for women.

Women's lives have been changing, as they have gained access to more education and they have enjoyed the economic independence that results from improved employment opportunities. One consequence of this is that women have been delaying the age at which they enter into marriage.

Another consequence is that more single women who have considerable economic resources feel that they are sufficiently financially stable to have children on their own, without having to rely on the income of a male provider. For single women whose reproductive years are drawing to a close, having a child on their own may be the only way in which they can experience the joys of motherhood. Despite the trend towards declining fertility, most women still want to have at least one child. Becoming a parent helps to provide meaning for their lives, and it gives them a sense of personal fulfilment.

10 Parenting

Parenting is a complex social experience that varies from time to time and in different places, and according to the particular family involved. Although it appears to be a natural, biologically given phenomenon, it is in fact socially constructed. It reflects the dominant ideas about children, and about relationships between parents and children, and these ideas in turn are influenced by the culture of a society and by its dominant social institutions. Formal education, for example, is a dominant social institution in modern society. The increasing domination of educational systems has transformed childhood and socialization in modern societies, and formal education shapes relationships between parents and children in profound ways. For one thing, the length of time that children spend in formal education means that children are an economic burden on their parents rather than an economic asset. In premodern societies, children were typically given tasks to perform that contributed to the family's economic and social well-being. With the introduction of formal education, however, children spend a considerable portion of their time in school or doing homework, and so they are less useful to their parents. This has implications for decisions that parents make about their children, such as deciding how many children to have. Children are expensive, and so economically rational parents decide to have fewer of them. In a society in which children have an economic value to the family, there is little need to restrict the number of children. But in a society in which children have no economic value, having fewer children is an attractive choice (Jensen, 1994). The dominance of formal education therefore has implications for fertility decisions.

Today, one of the principal attributes of the role of the parent is to prepare children for entry into school, and to support the work of the school so that children graduate with good marks. Parental stress on the educational achievements of their children reflects the pressures of other social institutions, such as the formal organizations in which most modern children will be employed when they become adults. Bureaucratic organizations conduct their hiring, and they sort their employees, partly on the basis of people's formal educational qualifications. It is therefore part of the responsibility of modern parents to prepare their children for the world of work, by providing the emotional, intellectual and financial support that will enable them to obtain the best education possible. This means that parents today must invest a lot of their resources, and themselves, in their children in a process of intensive parenting.

MODERN PARENTING

Intensive parenting is a historically constructed cultural model for appropriate childcare. Not only do the parents assume a relatively great responsibility for the development of their children, but mothers in particular are seen as playing the preponderant role in shaping how their children will grow up. This means that in most cases it is mothers rather than other adults who are believed to be the natural caregivers for children. In the United States, some of the crucial elements of the ideology of intensive mothering appeared in the middle classes in the late eighteenth and early nineteenth centuries (Hays, 1996). During this period, motherhood was valorized as an important status in its own right, parents went to great lengths to prolong the period of childhood innocence, and the mother–child relationship became suffused with affection. Child-rearing came to be understood as a task that was best done primarily by the mother, without the benefit of help from servants, older children or other women.

By the second half of the nineteenth century, child-rearing was synonymous with mothering, as women were entrusted with raising children while men were occupied in business and politics. The father was still the ultimate authority in family life, but the mother now had a much larger and more valued role to play in shaping the child. Mothers were held to stand at the centre of family life, as the guardians of moral virtue and as a bulwark against the corrupting influences of the outside world. During this era, mothers began to be represented as the keepers of morality whose responsibility it was to raise virtuous children. With this shift towards an image of the moral mother, the mother's role in child-rearing began to take on a new importance. The status of the mother depended increasingly on her careful rearing of a small number of children rather than on her fecundity. This enhanced role required a new emphasis on expertise in child-rearing. Because of their centrality in the child's world, it was thought that mothers should be educated for their role and an emphasis on instructing mothers developed. Mothers were encouraged to look to child experts for advice on child-rearing, and new, more scientific categories of child development were promulgated. A mother had to know all the latest information on the child's physical, emotional and cognitive development, and she had to be constantly attentive to her particular child's stage of development in order to do her job of child-rearing properly. The mother was instructed to bring all her knowledge, religious devotion and capacities for love to bear on the task of raising her children.

Part of the reason why women acquired a new importance in the lives of their children was because of their importance as keepers of the home. As the capitalist economy developed and production was moved outside the household, the home was constructed as a private sphere of domesticity separated from the public sphere of market transactions and state power. The home became separated from the outside world of industry, and it took on its own particular emotional flavour. It was valorized as warm and nurturing, and as a haven from the harsh realities of the market economy. The home came to be seen as a site of love and affection in contrast to the hard economic calculation of the business world. Women, as the homemakers, were the principal providers of this love and affection. The relationship between mothers and children therefore came to be one of affection, in which mothers sacrificed their own interests because of their love for their children. Children, in turn, were thought to inspire love because of their purity and innocence.

In the late eighteenth and early nineteenth centuries, children were increasingly portrayed as innocent beings who were uncorrupted as long as they were protected from the influences of the world outside the home. The child's world was therefore different from the adult world, and toys, games and books designed exclusively for children proliferated. It was thought that childhood innocence should be prolonged as long as possible, and childhood as a social construction became extended. At the same time, childhood was extended because of the felt necessity to provide for children a lengthy period of formal education that would prepare them for life in the modern world. The child who was once an economic asset was now provided with an increasingly costly period of protected education. Child labour laws and compulsory schooling meant that child-rearing had become expensive. Children not only needed the right toys, books and clothes, but they also had to be kept out of the paid labour force and supported while they were in school.

During the twentieth and early twenty-first centuries, average periods of formal education have become increasingly lengthy with the expansion of further education, and the ideology of intensive mothering has grown more extensive and elaborate. The emphasis on the bond between mother and child, the stress on the child's physical, psychological and cognitive development, and the belief in the importance of child experts all persist. Today, the child experts include psychologists, and ideas from popular psychology have permeated the culture (Frønes, 1997). The message of popular psychology is that parents mould their children to some extent, and it is therefore important for parents to take on responsibility for their child's development by providing a stimulating environment and encouraging activities that spur growth. This requires greater commitments of money and time from the parents. Passive time that parents used to spend with children, and the time that mothers spent on housework have decreased. The emphasis now is on parents spending 'quality time' with children.

The modern metaphor of 'quality time' signals the fact that parents are involved in their children's lives, and that they are concerned about their stimulation and development. Parents have taken an increasingly more active role in children's activities, and they have intervened more in children's lives. Parents now provide items like sports equipment, music education and other organized activities that are seen as enhancing the child's achievement potential. As they have done so, the level of children's participation in organized leisure activities has increased. This is partly in accordance with the ideas of popular psychology, partly because of growing worries about the dangers of the streets, and partly because of the trend in an educational society to organize children's lives more. Modern schooling confirms the need for active parenting, such as help with homework, and it stresses the role of the parents emphasized by popular psychology.

At the same time as there is continuity with the recent past with the extension of intensive mothering, the mother's relationship to the home has changed. The dominant type of family with children now involves both mother and father in pursuing their individual careers. Ivar Frønes has argued from data on Norway that this does not mean that egocentric parents cultivate their own careers at the expense of their children (Frønes, 1997). Children, and their development, remain at the heart of the family project. Of course, most mothers are no longer confined to a private sphere of domesticity, and they must balance their responsibilities in the home with their commitments to paid employment. An-Magritt Jensen, in a report on parent–child relationships in Scandinavia, concludes that as a result of changing employment patterns the amount of time in which parents are directly involved with children has declined (Jensen, 1998). As a result, young children spend more time with non-parental caregivers, and as they get older children are given greater autonomy. Parents expect their children to engage in more self-management, especially when older children are at home alone. As both parents have vacated the home, older children spend more time at home without parental supervision. This has given them greater control over the use of the family home and the time that they spend in it. However, there is a limit to this new-found autonomy. At the same time as children have gained more independence from their parents, mothers' expectations of children have changed. Working mothers expect more help from children with the housework, particularly if they are employed full-time. Children therefore take on a significant share of the housework in Scandinavia, and increasingly so as the children grow older.

Partly because of the new pressure of employment on mothers, a new emphasis has emerged on involving fathers in child-rearing. Employment among mothers has paved the way for new expectations of parenthood, including increased participation by fathers in childcare (Jensen, 1994). Such developments as encouraging fathers to be involved in prenatal care and to be present at the birth of their children have emerged as ways of attempting to strengthen the bond between father and child. Also, some countries offer fathers access to parental leave from work. This provides new fathers with paid leave, and the guarantee of re-employment at the end of the leave, in order to enable them to stay home with their newborn children (Højgaard, 1997). Some fathers take advantage of this policy whereas others do not. The main reason that many men do not avail themselves of parental leave is because of the consequences of absence from work in terms of losing influence in the workplace and consequently falling behind on the career ladder. To be committed to fatherhood is to have a marginal status in the labour market. This is especially a problem for men who define themselves as the main providers for their families.

Kathleen Gerson has argued from her research in the United States that fathers who do not follow the traditional family breadwinner model have moved in two contradictory directions (Gerson, 1994; 1997). On one hand, there are more men who have engaged in a flight from commitment, in which they have largely given up their responsibilities to parent and they have left women to raise their children in single-parent families. These men were likely to have encountered blocked opportunities at work, or to have become disillusioned with dead-end jobs, which led them to reject the idea of earning a family wage. Also, they were likely to have had difficulties in their relationships with women, and with children, in some cases culminating in emotional and economic estrangement from their children following family breakups. On the other hand, some men in relationships have moved towards more rather than less family involvement. In contrast to the traditional definition of family responsibilities by married men, which has stressed their role as family breadwinners, the latter men have included caregiving as well as economic support in their definition of fatherhood. They are changing diapers (or in other words, nappies), pushing strollers, cuddling their children, and generally sharing in the pleasures and burdens of child-rearing. These men are typically in relationships with women who are committed to their careers, and they have an egalitarian attitude towards family responsibilities. For these men, intensive mothering has evolved into intensive fathering.

According to Gerson, involved fathers are mainly men who have looked for meaning in their lives beyond the pursuit of money and prestige. In some cases, particularly among less-educated men who had fewer career opportunities, this was because of blocked aspirations for upward mobility. At the same time, these men had become involved with women who were committed to their work and who expected their partners to help carry the burdens of housework and childcare. Choosing wives who were committed to their work relieved these men of sole or primary responsibility for supporting families financially, and at the same time it gave their partners a greater desire and ability to secure male participation in child-rearing.

When a father's dissatisfaction with his job combined with a mother's growing work commitment, their life trajectories converged to make equal parenting or primary parenting by the father more attractive. Women's changing work commitments and expectations, as well as men's experiences, contributed to these men's redefinitions of their family roles. In some cases the partners of involved fathers had career opportunities better than or equal to their spouses, and therefore pushed for marital and parental equality. Equal fathers were more likely than fathers who were less involved in parenting to be in a relationship with a woman who had better long-term career prospects. As these men developed relationships with women who desired and expected help with child-rearing, and as they looked for meaning beyond the workplace, they found unexpected pleasure in parenting. Spending time with their children became as important to them as contributing money to the family economy.

Although some fathers have been increasing their time spent with children, others have been diminishing it. An increasing proportion of fathers have become distanced from their children, whether voluntarily or not. That is because one of the most fundamental changes in parent–child relations that has occurred in recent decades is the waning of the role of biological fathers, due to the dissolution of families with divorce and the tendency for children of divorce to stay with their mothers.

Involvement of non-resident fathers in their children's lives is typically low. The preponderance of data in the United States indicates that a high number of non-resident fathers disengage from their children when they do not live in the same household with them (Furstenberg, 1994). Many men regard parenthood as part of a 'package deal' that is inextricably linked with marriage or cohabitation. Men often relate to their children in large part through their wives or partners. The disintegration of that relationship therefore reduces non-custodial fathers' willingness to invest time and other resources in their children. The end result of all this is a paradox. A modern family pattern, which is driven in part by changing gender roles, has led to a strengthening of the traditional gender division concerning parental responsibilities for children. Only a small minority of children live with their fathers after dissolution of the parental relationship, and most children of divorce subsequently see their fathers infrequently. This has sparked an intense debate in the United States over the consequences for children of parental divorce (Cherlin, 1999).

Social scientists in the United States have attempted to study what are the consequences of marital disruption for children. The research findings are contradictory and have permitted various conclusions to be drawn. Nevertheless, the majority of studies show that the children of divorce are more likely to exhibit psychological, behavioural, social, and academic problems than children raised continuously in intact two-parent families (Amato, Loomis and Booth, 1995). We will consider this issue further in the next chapter. For now, we will turn to consider the contents of interactions between parents and children as these too have been changing.

NEGOTIATING CHILDHOOD

In the past, the focus of child-rearing was on ensuring the child's conformity to adult interests. Obedience was expected, and enforced. Beginning in the United States in the 1930s, however, the content of child-rearing became more permissive and more child-centred (Hays, 1996). Unvarying obedience was no longer considered desirable, as children were thought to need to find their own way in the world. Increasingly, it was felt that training to conform to adult interests and desires should not begin too early or be too strict. An emphasis on nurturing the child's inner nature replaced the stress on rigid behavioural training of the child to meet adult requirements. Parents came to be seen as responding to the needs and desires of children, rather than imposing adult choices upon them. The natural development of the child and the fulfilment of children's desires were now thought to be most important as the fundamental bases for child-rearing practices. For the first time, it was believed to be necessary to understand each child as an individual, and to adapt child-rearing practices to each child's pattern of development. This approach was reinforced by child-rearing manuals such as Dr Benjamin Spock's *Baby and Child Care*, that became popular after the Second World War. Spock's recommendations centered on the crucial importance of child-rearing that was founded on maternal affection, that followed from the child's development, and that allowed the child ample room to express its wants and needs. He argued for less rigid discipline, and he believed that mothers should follow the child's lead rather than demanding adult behaviour. This influential book signalled a shift in authority relationships between the parent and the child, away from the imposition of parental authority and towards the negotiation of childhood.

Peter Büchner and his colleagues have hypothesized that this shift in authority relations was the result of changes occurring in the Western societies as they underwent continued modernization (Büchner, Krüger and du Bois-Reymond, 1994). Modern societies increasingly emphasize decision-making by individuals as they make their way in an open market economy. There are increased opportunities and freedom of choice for those who can take advantage of them, and educational and labour market institutions therefore stress individual success and encourage competitiveness. This is reflected in changes in social relationships. The interests, ambitions and commitments of individuals have become the focus of attention rather than group solidarity. This process of 'individualization' affects not only adults, but it also affects the lives of children and consequently their relationships with their parents.

In those families which have been most affected by the modernizing process, children must take responsibility for themselves from an early age as they prepare to enter an individualized adult world. Parents tend to focus more on children as individuals, and to encourage them to develop their individuality. Partly this is because of the trend of families to become smaller, as a result of which the individual child comes to be of greater importance. In a family where there are fewer children, and therefore more time to give attention to the individual child, a greater intimacy develops between parents and children and the parent becomes more interested in the child's development.

The development of each child's interests and abilities becomes the criterion of successful child-rearing, and children are to a certain extent able to seek their own pursuits regardless of parental preferences. Because modern children are regarded as individuals in their own right, parents show more sensitivity to children's wants and needs and aim to accept and foster the child's autonomy, self-regulation and self-control.

Children are expected to control themselves more and to need fewer external controls, and coercive measures to suppress undesired behaviour are therefore no longer favoured as a child-rearing strategy. Attempts to influence children's behaviour through corporal punishment are replaced by efforts to guide children's choices by pointing out to them the consequences of their actions. In this socialization process, children acquire experience in making choices that will influence the lines along which their lives develop. The main aim of giving children autonomy at an early age is to give children the ability to make choices, and to be confident in their own preferences.

One of the most prominent features of an individualized childhood is the child's early acquisition of independence in a range of activities. Parents today concede more freedom to their children than they enjoyed themselves when they were children. In a study of parent–child relationships in the Netherlands, the majority of mothers and fathers stated that they brought up their children along more liberal lines than those in which they were brought up themselves (du Bois-Reymond, 1995). Examples of areas of independence enjoyed by modern children include planning and managing the child's space in the home, choosing what to buy, selecting leisure activities, expressing personal tastes in clothing, and determining media consumption patterns. The modern child thus develops an orientation towards self-realization as opposed to fulfilling obligations to others. As a result, relationships between many parents and children are not primarily guided by traditional norms and values, fixed standards of socialization, or authority arising from parental status. Rather, parent–child relationships are open for negotiation. In those families most affected by the modernizing process, relationships between parents and children have changed in recent decades from a basic pattern of authority–obedience relations to a pattern of recurrent negotiation between parents and children. According to Manuela du Bois-Reymond, there is an ongoing development towards a culture of negotiation in family life, which is typical of modern society (du Bois-Reymond, 1995).

Negotiation is a pattern of communication that implies equal partnership. Parent and child each present their definitions of the situation, and themselves, and children as well as parents are responsible for articulating their points of view and for reaching agreement on a line of action. Children therefore develop the communicative skills that they will require in adult life when they must negotiate their way through complex situations. They learn at an early age to manage their everyday lives by negotiating in a civilized way with their partners in interaction, beginning with their parents. This modern type of parenting takes the form of a relatively democratic parent–child relationship which is believed to foster the child's autonomy, self-confidence, self-control and capacity for decision-making.

Of course, this modern approach to parenting is not found in all families, and its prevalence varies by age, with older children having more autonomy than younger children. Recent research suggests that today there exist notable class differences in parenting styles. Manuela du Bois-Reymond reports from a study of young people in The Netherlands that the traditional emphasis on parents laying down the rules and expecting their children to follow them no matter what is now found mainly in the lower classes (du Bois-Reymond, 1995). Yet, even here, parents are today more likely to discuss issues with their children than they would have been in previous generations. The upper and middle classes appear to have been most affected by the changes associated with modernization, as these families are more likely to have negotiating family cultures. Upper-class young people today have a better chance of growing up in a family that practises negotiation between parents and children than do young people from the lower classes, although the latter too now enjoy more autonomy than they had in the past. It appears that at the present time upper-class families are leading the trend towards new roles for children in their relationships with their parents.

DISCUSSION

Childhood and parenthood have been changing in the past couple of centuries, and especially in recent decades. Parents have acquired a greater responsibility for determining how their children turn out, reflecting ideas of popular psychology which stress the influence that parents have over their children's development. Parents are perceived as the primary influence in their children's lives, and parents therefore carry a great responsibility for shaping their children's entry into a successful adulthood. With the advent of capitalism, this responsibility was seen as falling overwhelmingly on the shoulders of mothers, as fathers were engaged in earning the family income in the market economy. The result was an ideology of intensive mothering, which placed the mother at the centre of the child's world and assigned to mothers the duty of providing a secure and protected home environment based on expressions of the mother's love. Subsequently, the idea has developed that fathers as well as mothers should be involved in their children's lives. Intensive mothering has become an egalitarian intensive parenting in some families. Nevertheless, mothers still retain the primary responsibility for childcare in most cases.

Family roles have not only become more egalitarian as regards the division of responsibilities between mothers and fathers, but they have also become more egalitarian as regards relationships between parents and children. Although class differences persist, the trend has been unmistakably towards less authoritarian styles of parenting. This trend has culminated in the pattern found in some families of parents and children negotiating with each other over their respective lines of action. Partly this trend reflects increasing uncertainty felt by parents over how best to prepare their children for a changing world. But it also is partly shaped by the idea that children need to be prepared to exercise greater autonomy in their lives, in a modern society in which the children's well-being as adults will depend increasingly upon the decisions they make about crucial events in their life course.

In all these changes in parent–child relations, the changing lives of women have had a great influence. Mothers now work outside the home in much greater numbers, beginning when their children are relatively young. In order to meet both their family responsibilities and their employment responsibilities, mothers need more help from both their partners and their children. This has put increased pressure upon fathers to participate actively in raising their children, and it has put more pressure upon older children to manage their lives responsibly without as much direct parental supervision, and to help out their mothers with the housework. As parents' lives have changed, so too have the lives of children.

11 Family transformations

Changes in family relationships occur as macro-sociological changes in historical time, which take place over decades and centuries, but they also occur as micro-sociological changes during the lives of family members. Changes such as births, divorce or leaving home all have their impact on family life, just as much as changes such as the advent of capitalism or increased employment of mothers. At one time it was thought that these life course changes took the form of a predictable sequence of family events known as the family lifecycle. Family life begins with marriage, proceeds through childbearing and child-rearing to be followed eventually by the children leaving home, and culminates in the end of the family when the partners die. Or so it was thought. Today we recognize that there is no predictable sequence of family events. Some people follow the pattern of the family lifecycle, but many do not. Couples may cohabit before getting married, or they may live together without ever marrying, and they may separate or get divorced thus dissolving the family prior to the death of one of the partners. People who get divorced may subsequently remarry, forming new families and, if there are children involved, they create new sets of step-relationships. All of these complexities mean that family events must be studied individually, rather than as part of a sequence of role changes.

DIVORCE

In an earlier chapter we discussed family formation through marriage, cohabitation and childbearing. In this chapter we will examine the opposite process, namely the process of family dissolution. One way in which families are dissolved is through divorce. In the last third of the twentieth century, divorce increased substantially in most developed nations. However, in some developing nations, notably in the Muslim world of Southeast Asia, divorce rates have actually fallen. In West Java,

Indonesia, for example, divorce rates were falling at the same time as they were rising in the West (Jones, Asari and Djuartika, 1994). Part of the reason for this is that the divorce rate in Indonesia in general, and West Java in particular, was historically higher than it was in the West. Traditionally, divorce in West Java was easy to obtain and there was no particular stigma attached to it. Where spouses were not able to resolve the initial period of adapting to one another, divorce was a socially acceptable means of rectifying the situation with no social sanction attached to the dissolution of the relationship. In fact, divorce was a readily available solution to certain fundamental problems in the institution of marriage. Marriages occurred at an early age and were often arranged. Where the bride discovered that she did not like the bridegroom she would often refuse to consummate the marriage, and divorce would follow soon afterwards. Also, being young, the bride and groom often lacked social maturity and found it difficult to make the adjustments that marriage entails. The combination of relatively high tensions at the onset of marriage and the easy availability of divorce meant that many marriages were quickly dissolved. Divorce in West Java, compared with other societies, has traditionally been more likely to take place soon after marriage.

In recent decades changes have occurred in West Java in particular, and in Indonesia as a whole, as a result of which divorce rates have declined (Guest, 1992; Heaton, Cammack and Young, 2001). As in other parts of the world, there has been a rise in average age at marriage. This has meant that young people are now more mature when they get married, and therefore they are better able to cope with the adjustments of marriage. Age at marriage in Indonesia is negatively related to the probability of divorce (Guest, 1992). Another factor reducing the tensions associated with the early stages of marriage has been a decline in arranged marriages, and an accompanying trend for young people to choose their own partners on the basis of personal preference. A lesser tendency for parents to arrange marriages may be related in turn to increased education of women and their greater employment outside the home, which may have given young women greater autonomy from their parents. At the same time, young women have had increased contact with the opposite sex in school and at the workplace, which has made possible the development of affectionate relationships leading to marriage. Previously, the general social disapproval of mixing adolescent males and females led to situations in which spouses were in many respects strangers, even when they might have been from the same village. Another factor encouraging lower divorce rates has been changes in divorce laws and regulations which have made divorce harder to obtain.

Some of the sharpest declines in divorce in West Java appear to be correlated with the introduction of new laws, or of new procedures for implementing these laws. Official attitudes towards divorce have been negative, and on balance divorce has been made more time-consuming and costly to obtain, thus increasing the disincentive to divorce.

Although divorce rates have fallen in Islamic Southeast Asia, the trend in Western societies has been in the opposite direction. In the West, changes in divorce laws have made divorce easier to obtain. These legal changes have been partly in response to an increased demand for divorce, but there is no doubt that they have also been a factor which has facilitated increased divorce rates. In recent decades, the rate of increase of divorce and the prevalence of marital disruption were both highest in the United States. The incidence of divorce and the proportion of children affected by divorce have been higher in the USA than in any other industrialized country. We will therefore pay special attention to divorce in the United States.

Frank Furstenberg speculates that the increase in divorce and its high prevalence in the United States are partly due to the expansion of an individualistic culture that emphasizes individual choice as well as personal freedom and self-actualization (Furstenberg, 1994). Americans are less constrained to divorce because in large numbers they endorse values of freedom of action. At the same time, the expectations of marriage are high and may have risen. Western family systems in general, and the United States in particular, place a high premium on finding happiness in marriage, resulting in a desire to end the relationship if that happiness is not found. This has been coupled with a shift in the meaning of marriage away from a gender-based division of labour, in which men were committed to paid employment in order to earn a family wage and women specialized in child-rearing and domestic activity. As a result, it is possible that women's expectations of marriage have changed, as working wives expect more egalitarian marriages. This may have led to more marital discontent when their husbands have not changed. Also, with the increase in the number of women employed outside the home, most wives now depend less upon their husbands and they are not forced to stay in unsatisfactory marriages for economic reasons. Most Americans, perhaps women especially, are now less willing than they once were to settle for passable marriages, because they have the option of living alone in the event that such relationships do not work out. A high rate of marital dissolution in the United States is the result of a combination of extremely high standards for intimate relationships and the widespread availability of social and economic alternatives for those who do not achieve the desired standard of marital happiness.

Of course, not all marriages end in divorce. In fact, only a minority of marriages do so. It is therefore possible to ask what are the factors associated with marital disruption, and what are the factors associated with staying married. A recent Canadian study has examined this issue (Clark and Crompton, 2006). Participation in organized religion is one factor associated with the probability of divorce. Religious observance is associated with marital durability, whereas not attending religious services is associated with a greater likelihood of marital dissolution. Another factor is age at marriage. The younger people are when they get married, the more likely it is that the marriage will be dissolved prior to death. Presumably this is because people who marry at older ages are more mature and therefore are better able to cope with the adjustments required of marriage. It is also possible that marital stability is related to economic security, and generally speaking the older people are, the more economically secure they are also. A third factor associated with marital stability and instability is education. The less education people have, the greater is the risk of marital dissolution. This is consistent with evidence that people with higher socioeconomic status tend to be happier on average and are less likely to divorce. Finally, there is a growing body of evidence that marital instability is related to the experience of having cohabited before marriage. Cohabitation before marriage is strongly associated with the risk of marital breakdown. This may be because the tradition of marriage is less important to people who have participated in non-traditional conjugal relationships, but there may also be other reasons.

The discovery that there is a strong negative association between premarital cohabitation and marital stability is one of the more puzzling findings in family sociology in recent years. The popular belief is that living together before marrying gives people a chance to try out their relationship and test their commitment to one another. Relationships that do not work very well are dissolved with no marriage having taken place, and presumably those relationships that survive and lead to marriage should be more stable. Living together before marrying should therefore be an effective way to reduce a couple's chance of divorcing. But that is not what has been found. Couples who live together prior to marriage are more likely to see their relationship break up than are couples who get married without cohabiting.

David Hall has hypothesized that the negative association found between premarital cohabitation and marital stability is due to the nature of the relationship between cohabiting couples (Hall, 1996). People who live together before marriage, in contrast to people who begin their conjugal life with marriage, are less committed to the institution of marriage and are more committed to a type of relationship that Hall, following Anthony Giddens, refers to as a pure relationship. A pure relationship is one in which the partners develop the strength of their bond out of their own interactions rather than from externally imposed constraints. These relationships are therefore organized and sustained primarily from the value that they have for the participants. They are not based on external social forces such as norms, traditions or formal institutions. Instead, they are maintained by the partners on the basis of the relationship's capacity to realize their self-actualization. If the relationship does not lead to self-actualization, then it can be dissolved. Pure relationships can therefore be terminated, more or less at will, by either partner at any time.

Supporting evidence for this thesis is presented by David Hall from the Canadian Fertility Survey. He found that attitudes towards pure relationships are significantly associated with the probability of divorce. Women who eschew pure relationships have a risk of divorce that is much lower than those who highly approve of pure relationships. Furthermore, when attitudes towards pure relationships are statistically controlled, premarital cohabitation no longer predicts divorce. It follows that favourable views on pure relationships account for the high risk of marital instability associated with premarital cohabitation.

Consequences of divorce

If the incidence of pure relationships in modern society has grown, as indicated by Giddens, then this might help to explain the increase in divorce rates. Increased divorce rates may be attributed partly to changing expectations of marriage, with more being demanded of marriage partners in contemporary society. Or, they may be partly due to the increased tendency for economically independent women to claim greater autonomy for themselves. Either way, one of the noteworthy aspects of this process is that single-parent families, usually single-mother families, have become a more noticeable feature of the landscape of childhood. An-Magritt Jensen has referred to this process as part of 'the feminization of childhood' (Jensen, 1994). Because many mothers who are divorced eventually remarry, at any given time there are relatively few children living in single-mother families. However, an increasing proportion of children experience part of their childhood in this family form. The main reason for this is divorce, as most single-parent families are formed as the result of the dissolution of a union rather than as the result of extra-marital childbearing or the death of a partner. Studying the effects on children of living in single-parent families therefore tells us something about the consequences of divorce.

Sara McLanahan has argued that growing up in a single-mother family is disadvantageous for children (McLanahan, 1994). She believes the research evidence shows that children who grow up with only one of their biological parents (nearly always the mother) do not do as well as children who grow up with both biological parents. Children of single parents in the United States have lower grade point averages in school, lower college aspirations, and poorer school attendance records. They are also more likely to drop out of school, and after leaving school they are more likely to be out of work, while girls are more likely to become mothers themselves in adolescence. McLanahan concludes that the evidence strongly suggests that family disruption plays a causal role in lowering children's well-being.

The effect of family disruption in lowering children's well-being may be because single-parent families have lower incomes than intact two-parent families, and when parents live apart children therefore have less income available to them. Marital disruption causes an abrupt decline in household income, and this pattern has not changed over time (Smock, 1993). Divorce therefore typically results in a decline in the standard of living of mothers and their children. This is partly due to the loss of economies of scale in a smaller family, but it is mostly because non-custodial fathers pay little or no child support (Hanson, McLanahan and Thomson, 1998). Family disruption may also lower children's well-being because most children of divorce see less of their fathers, who are therefore less able to influence and control them. The most obvious direct effect of divorce is the sharp reduction in contact between children and non-custodial parents. And finally, the negative effects of family disruption on children's well-being may arise from the fact that divorce often sets in motion events that can be stressful for children, such as moving, changing schools, and parental remarriage. Residential mobility, for example, can weaken ties to friends and kin and therefore reduce community resources available to sustain effective parent–child relationships.

Bob Coles concludes from the available research in Britain that there is some cause for concern about the consequences for children of trends in family structure (Coles, 1995). The number of young people being brought up in families in which they will experience divorce, being brought up by single parents, and joining reconstituted families has grown. Coles believes the research evidence indicates that the material and emotional circumstances of such children suffer and that, as a result, their educational performance and school qualifications are not as high.

For example, British children who do not live in an intact family leave school at an earlier age.

In a more detailed study in the Netherlands, it was also found that the educational attainment of children from single-mother families and families with a step-father is lower than that of children from families with both biological parents present (Dronkers, 1994). The poorer school performance of children from single-parent families cannot be explained by the greater tendency of single-parent families to exhibit certain characteristics which are unfavourable to educational attainment, such as lower education of single mothers. After controlling for these negative characteristics, significant differences remain between the educational attainments of children from single-parent families and children from intact two-parent families. It appears that children who are separated from their biological fathers do not do as well as children who remain with them.

One controversial aspect of the consequences of divorce for children is whether or not those consequences persist into adulthood. The balance of the evidence from American studies suggests that adults who experienced parental divorce as children have lower psychological well-being, lower socioeconomic attainment, and poorer-quality marital relationships than adults who were raised in intact two-parent families. However, it is possible that only part of these relationships is due to divorce itself, and part is due to the pre-divorce characteristics of families which dissolve through divorce, such as marital conflict. Children do less well in families where there is a great deal of conflict, and problems for children of divorce are often apparent before marital dissolution. If divorce of a conflicting couple ends the conflict relationship, does this mean that divorce can sometimes have a beneficial effect for children? Research by Paul Amato, Laura Spencer Loomis and Alan Booth suggests so.

In a study of young adults in the United States, Amato and his colleagues found that the consequences of parental divorce in childhood depend upon how much conflict there was between the parents prior to divorce (Amato, Loomis and Booth, 1995). Where parental conflict had been high, children had higher levels of well-being as young adults if their parents divorced than if they stayed together. But if there had been little conflict between the parents, children had higher levels of well-being if their parents stayed together than if they divorced. Or to put it the other way round, psychological well-being and the quality of intimate relations were found to be lowest when low marital conflict is followed by divorce as well as when high marital conflict is not followed by divorce. This suggests that changes in family structure (i.e. divorce) and family processes (i.e. conflict) interact to affect children's well-being in adulthood. The data support the conclusion that the long-term consequences of divorce depend upon the level of parental conflict prior to separation. Children are therefore better off in single-parent families than in two-parent families marked by high levels of discord, but they are better off in two-parent families than in single-parent families if there is little parental conflict.

HOME LEAVING

To this point, we have considered divorce as a way in which family relationships are transformed. Another way in which family relationships are transformed is when children leave home to live independently. Sometimes relationships are terminated upon home leaving, usually as a result of family conflict. More often, however, relationships are continued but interactions change in frequency and nature. The nature of relationships after home leaving probably varies according to whether the adult children leave for positive reasons or negative reasons. Young adults may leave home for positive reasons such as going to college or university, or in order to obtain employment. Or, they may leave home for negative reasons such as a desire to avoid friction with parents or step-parents.

One of the sociological questions that has been examined about home leaving is whether it varies according to the history of family relationships and the social structure of the home that is being left. The available data suggest that there is a relationship between these factors. Studies in Britain, for example, suggest that children are more likely to leave home early if they have experienced family disruption (Coles, 1995). In particular, having a step-parent is the main predictive correlate of leaving home early. Young women from step-families, and young men who have experienced family disruption, are also more likely to leave home for negative reasons, with the notable exception of young men living with lone mothers. It seems likely that discipline from step-parents is experienced as particularly problematic by young people, who often regard it as illegitimate. Young people's reaction to the difficulties they experience in step-families is to leave home (often for negative reasons) earlier than young people from intact families.

Similar data are available from the United States, Canada and Sweden. In Sweden it has been found that adolescents and young adults have elevated odds of leaving home earlier in life if their parental home was disrupted during childhood (Bernhardt, Gähler and Goldscheider, 2005). Also, young men and women from disrupted families are more likely to leave home to enter a union than those who grow up in intact families, and they are more likely to leave home for residential independence if their families are disrupted than if they are not. In contrast, there is no effect of family disruption on leaving home to attend school for either young women or young men. Family conflict and having a step-parent affect age of leaving the parental home, and family disruption has no effect on home leaving if there is neither conflict nor a step-parent.

In the United States and Canada it has been found that children living in step-families and single-parent families leave home sooner than children who live with both biological parents (Mitchell, Wister and Burch, 1989; Aquilino, 1991; Zhao, Rajulton and Ravanera, 1995). This relationship is particularly strong for young women who have grown up in step-families. Research with step-families has provided the strongest evidence of a linkage between family structure and children's home leaving, as living in a single-parent household has a weaker impact on home leaving than growing up with a step-parent. It is also worth noting that William Aquilino finds for the USA that the impact of living in a single-parent family upon home leaving varies according to the stability of family structure in childhood (Aquilino, 1991). The home leaving of children who have lived in single-parent families from birth does not differ from the pattern for those who lived in intact families. This suggests that it is the stability or instability of childhood family structure, rather than the type of family structure, that influences the timing of home leaving.

As in Britain, the effect of living in step-families upon home leaving in the United States is usually attributed to more problematic parent–child relations in families containing step-parents. Step-children, for example, are more likely than other children to cite conflict with parents as a reason for leaving home. It is also possible that parents in step-families are more likely to encourage their children to leave home early, as a solution to the marital difficulties brought on by conflicts over how to bring up the children. Parents in step-families in the USA expect children to live independently at an earlier stage in life than parents in intact families.

The relationship between family structure and reasons for home leaving also seems to be similar in the United States and Britain. Living in a step-family not only increases the chances of early home leaving, but it also increases the likelihood that home leavers will marry or live independently outside marriage rather than leaving for educational purposes. According to William Aquilino, exposure to non-intact family structures increases the probability of an early transition to residential independence and decreases the likelihood of leaving home to attend school (Aquilino, 1991).

DISCUSSION

In this chapter we have studied two ways in which family relationships are disrupted or attenuated, namely divorce and home leaving by children. Although divorce has decreased in some societies, such as those of the Muslim world of Southeast Asia, it has increased in the Western societies where most research on divorce has been conducted. Analysts have theorized about the causes of divorce, such as the growth of an individualistic culture, and they have especially examined the consequences of divorce for children. The effects of divorce upon children are usually described as being negative, as children who grow up without two biological parents tend to have lower educational attainments, for example. They are also more likely to leave home early, and to leave for reasons other than pursuing educational opportunities.

In some cases, early home leaving seems to be related to the presence of conflict in the family. Here the fact of home leaving is likely to be followed by a significant reduction in the frequency and intensity of contact between parents and children. In other cases, however, strong relationships are maintained after children leave home. Family relationships are not confined to relationships between people living in the same household, but family members living in different households frequently maintain substantial material and emotional ties. This points to the enduring importance of kinship ties in modern societies.

12 Kinship

The concept of kinship refers to the way in which social groups define relationships on the basis of marriage, descent and parenting. Kinship is a social relationship not a biological relationship, as we can see in the case of children who are adopted and raised as the parents' own child. People in one's kinship network are those who are recognized socially as kin, not necessarily those who have a genetic relationship. Kinship ties can be defined in different ways in different cultures, and as a result there have been many kinds of kinship structures. The tracing of lines of descent is one of the ways in which kinship structures have varied. In some societies descent is traced mainly through the female line (matrilineal kinship). In other societies, descent is traced mainly through the male line (patrilineal kinship). In traditional societies it can make a great deal of difference to people's lives whether kinship is patrilineal or matrilineal. That is because in traditional societies kinship has sometimes been the main basis on which social relationships are organized. However, over time the relative importance of kinship ties has declined. In modern societies, kinship is just one basis of social organization, along with such factors as the state, which we discuss in the next chapter.

In some societies, kinship has not only been the basis for providing people with a network of relationships, but it has also been the main criterion for assigning people into groups. Where kinship is a major basis of social organization, kinship groups tend to be formed whose members act together in a variety of contexts and, as a result, kinship group membership is the major determinant of an individual's rights, obligations and opportunities. Corporate kinship groups may control property in common, act as political units, and have their own particular religious rituals. An example of a corporate kinship group was the traditional Palestinian 'hamula'. The hamula was organized by tracing lines of descent through the male line. It consisted of a number of households whose male heads were linked to one another by descent from a common male ancestor. These households were usually placed in close proximity in the same village. Each hamula had a head, who was usually the oldest male. He made decisions for his wives and children, as well as his younger brothers and their wives and children, and his unmarried sisters. The head of the hamula arranged the distribution of land on which the members of the hamula grew their food, and he represented the hamula in its political relationships with external powers. In addition to making major economic and political decisions, the head of the hamula also had the major say about family relationships. This included making decisions on the choice of marriage partners for the children of the hamula, as well as decisions on divorce.

Among the Palestinians, kinship ties have changed over time and traditional structures have been modified. For example, most Palestinians no longer live in traditional hamulas, and more of them live in nuclear families like those found in the West. Still, modified hamula ties continue to be important for many Palestinians, especially in rural regions and in urban political organization in Israel.

MODIFIED EXTENDED FAMILY

Kinship ties continue to be important today. In modern societies such as the United States people frequently have family get-togethers, they telephone their relatives regularly, and they provide their kin with a wide variety of services. Eugene Litwak has referred to this pattern of behaviour as the 'modified extended family' (Litwak, 1960). It is an extended family structure because multigenerational ties are maintained, but it is modified because it does not usually rest on co-residence between the generations and most extended families do not act as corporate groups. Although modified extended family members often live close by, the modified extended family does not require geographical propinquity and ties are maintained even when kin are separated by considerable distances. In contrast to the traditional extended family where kin always live in close proximity, the members of modified extended families may freely move away from kin to seek opportunities for occupational advancement.

One of the noteworthy changes in the trend towards the modified extended family in Western societies has been a decline in co-residence between the generations. Although it seems unlikely that a majority of households in these societies were ever multigenerational households, the tendency has been for the number of people living in households spanning three or four generations to decrease. In the United States, for example, the proportion of households that were extended was relatively stable for most of the past century, but then it declined after the Second World War (Ruggles, 1994b). Steven Ruggles has argued that extended family households cannot have been very prevalent in the past for demographic reasons such as high fertility (large numbers of children) and high mortality (few elderly parents). Taking these factors into account, he has examined the proportion of elderly people residing with kin. He concludes that in America a century ago the majority of the elderly lived with their children, whereas that is no longer the case. In nineteenth-century America there were far too few elderly to create a majority of multigenerational families, but multigenerational living was still the ideal. Of course, there were significant racial differences. The long-run decline of multigenerational family structure has been much slower among non-Whites than among Whites and it continues to be higher among non-Whites today. However, the decline among non-Whites has still been substantial. Multigenerational family living was the preferred family form a century ago, among both Whites and non-Whites, but residence patterns of both groups have changed. Co-residence of elderly parents with the younger generation was the norm in the past, but that is not the case today. Nevertheless, extended family ties have been maintained despite physical separation.

In modern, Western societies, relations between kin who live apart are made possible by advanced transportation and communications technologies. Despite the availability of these technologies, however, distance does make a difference to interaction patterns. With greater distance, contact, communication and mutual aid become less frequent. For this reason, extended family members prefer to live close together, and most parents live near and have frequent contact with at least some of their children. Urban living, which is a feature of modern society, may actually reduce people's need to migrate in search of employment, and hence increase their chances of living near kin, because of the range of occupational opportunities available in cities.

According to Howard Bahr, Jean-Hugues Déchaux and Karin Stiehr, the main characteristics of the modified extended family are: frequent interaction; close affective bonds; exchange of goods and services; mutual aid; voluntary interaction; and at least some family members residing within visiting distance (Bahr, Déchaux and Stiehr, 1994). Norms exist concerning obligations to help family members who are not resident in the same household. Most individuals feel obliged to help out if close relatives need help. At the same time, there are strong norms of non-interference and respect for the boundaries between family members who live in separate households. Parents are reluctant to get too involved in the affairs of their adult offspring who have established their own households and have children of their own.

Another characteristic of the modified extended family is that kinship structure is typically bilateral, meaning that descent is traced equally through the male and female lines. However, not all family members are deemed worthy of aid. Kinship bonds that skip a generation, as is true of grandparents and grandchildren, have a lesser priority. People feel the greatest commitment to assist primary kin, that is children and parents. Following as persons to be helped are relatives linked through these primary bonds, beginning with children-in-law, followed by grand-children and grandparents. Immediate kinship ties are emphasized, with a special focus upon relations between parents and their adult children.

Because mortality rates are low and longevity has increased, most parents spend a long period of their life course as the parent of an adult child. Relationships between older parents and their adult children are therefore an increasingly important focus of attention on intergenerational interaction within families. In economically advanced societies, most provision of support between the generations no longer takes the form of co-residence, but it involves emotional support, financial transfers and assistance with the practical tasks of daily living that go on between family members who are physically separated. In Britain and elsewhere parents tend to provide more help for children than children provide for parents, although in old age exchanges of support tend to become more balanced and may even be in favour of the elderly (Grundy, 2005). Ariela Lowenstein and Svein Olav Daatland report from a cross-national study of Norway, the United Kingdom, Germany, Spain and Israel that in advanced old age instrumental help flows upwards to the older generation but, when pension levels and living conditions allow, financial support flows downwards to the younger generation (Lowenstein and Daatland, 2006). Research on intergenerational transfers of wealth in the United States reveals that the flow of interhousehold gifts and transfers is overwhelmingly downward, from older ages to younger ones (Elmelech, 2005). However, level of economic development and attendant opportunities to acquire financial resources for old age, and the relative development of the welfare state, would seem to be factors affecting the direction of intergenerational transfers. For example, income from relatives, mainly adult children, is the primary source of income for the majority of older people in the Philippines, Thailand, Taiwan and Singapore (Agree, Biddlecom and Valente, 2005).

Parents and children engage in exchanges of support because they have shared the experience of living together, and this gives rise to a mutual interest in each other's well-being and a history of relationships which can endure physical separation. The tie between mother and child is especially close and it matters more than other kinship ties in terms of communication, caring, visiting and mutual aid. This reflects culturally defined gender roles, and the special place that most women have in nurturing activities. Women typically have a greater responsibility for maintaining kinship ties than men, and services provided for the elderly by kin other than spouses are usually provided by daughters and daughters-in-law, and to a lesser extent by sisters. Grandmothers are closer to their grandchildren than are grandfathers, and this is especially the case when daughters are in the middle generation (Aldous, 1995). As a result of this female bias in the kinship structure, paternal grandparents are generally less important in the lives of their descendants through the male line than are maternal grandparents who are connected to their grandchildren through the female line. If there is a divorce and the mother receives custody, as is usually the case, the paternal grandparent–grandchild connection is likely to become very weak. Grandparents of sons' children may lose contact with their grandchildren, who are likely to be in the custody of their daughters-in-law following divorce.

Relationships between mothers and daughters may be especially important if the daughters get divorced, when assistance is needed with such family functions as childcare. Grandparents, usually grandmothers, often look after their grandchildren so that the children's mothers can go out to work and engage in other activities. Divorce in the younger generation is not only a context for providing support between the generations, but it also poses challenges to the maintenance of social ties. It is therefore interesting to ask what is the effect of divorce on kinship ties.

Janet Finch and Jennifer Mason have examined this issue in a study of relationships between former in-laws after divorce and remarriage in Britain (Finch and Mason, 1990b). Their interest was especially in the extent to which ex-daughters-in-law care for elderly persons following divorce from their sons. Daughters-in-law are known to play a crucial role in the care of elderly parents, second only to daughters, and the question is whether this caring role continues after divorce. Finch and Mason's survey research showed considerable support in principle for the idea of maintaining the flow of mutual aid between mothers-in-law and daughters-in-law following divorce. In practice, however, few ex-in-laws provide support for each other. Most responses to divorce vary from cutting off relationships completely to maintaining good relations but without practical support. The process of ending a marriage tends to disrupt relations between in-laws, even when they had previously been very warm and close.

It is possible that divorce among older persons has the same effect as divorce in the younger generation in terms of attenuating kinship ties. Divorce undermines kinship support by disrupting exchanges and changing the normative context of social ties. With marriage the individual's effective kinship network expands by adding on the spouse's kin, whereas with divorce the effective kinship network contracts as the individual loses contact with his or her ex-in-laws. Sara Curran, Sara McLanahan and Jean Knab have examined this issue for elderly people in the United States of America (Curran, McLanahan and Knab, 2003). They find, as modified extended family theory would predict, that Americans are highly likely to turn to kin when they are in need of help. Elderly people are much more likely to turn to kin than friends, co-workers or neighbours for emergency support, emotional support and financial support. The authors also find that the effects of marital disruption on perceived support from kin are negative. Those who are divorced are less likely to turn to kin for support when they are in need. It is also noteworthy that divorce has more negative effects on men's perceptions of emergency, emotional and financial support than it does on women's perceptions of support. That is presumably because married men tend to rely on their wives to be the kinkeepers in their families, and they therefore lose more social support when they get divorced and are separated from their spouse's kin. Divorce reduces perceptions of support from kin in all domains for both men and women, but it has the greatest effect on men. Men benefit more from marriage in terms of kinship support and lose more from divorce than women.

EXTENDED FAMILY HOUSEHOLDS

As we have seen, kinship studies in Western societies have tended to focus on social support between non-co-resident kin, as extended kin tend not to live together. In Canada, for example, only 2.5 per cent of individuals aged 15 and over, and 3 per cent of grandparents, reside in a three-generation household (Kemp, 2003). However, outside Western societies co-residence among extended kin is more common, and the extended family household has therefore been a subject of some interest. In recent years, this interest has focused especially on societies in East Asia. Here, extended family co-residence remains an important feature of the social landscape in both urban and rural areas. In India, for example, there continues to be a preference for joint families, defined as families consisting of a household head and at least one married son or daughter and their spouse, or families containing two or more married brothers or sisters and their spouses (Niranjan, Nair and Roy, 2005).

Traditionally, one of the reasons for joint family preference in India was so that its members could own property in common, especially land. Maintenance of a piece of agricultural land required more resources and more labour, and hence the families who possessed agricultural land preferred to stay in joint families. On the other hand, where there was no land ownership and the standard of living was low, parents preferred their children to set up independent residence upon reaching marriageable age in order to lessen the demand upon household resources. There is still some evidence of this pattern today. A significantly high proportion of families are of the joint type if they own agricultural land compared with those who do not own any agricultural land. As a result, family structure in India is related to the system of stratification.

Analysis of family type according to standard of living indicates that higher proportions of joint families are more commonly seen among families with higher standards of living. Conversely, more families with a low standard of living are nuclear. Related to this is the fact that family structure is related to caste position. Families of the joint type are more often found among the higher castes compared with the lower castes, and families of the nuclear type are more common among the lower castes compared with the higher castes. However, it is worth noting that differences in family structure cannot be attributed to caste alone. That is because people from the lower castes who have acquired a high level of education, and who as a result have agricultural land and a high standard of living, have been more likely to adopt the joint family system than other members of the same caste. Caste is not a strong predictor of family structure independent of agricultural land-owning status and economic status of the family. Differences in family structure between the castes are therefore partly due to economic resources and landholding within the castes.

Despite the continuing preference for the joint family under certain conditions, there are more nuclear families than there are joint families in India today. Living in joint families has been declining and nuclear family living has been increasing over the past two decades. The joint family system is continuing in India but in lower percentages when compared with nuclear families. The shift away from joint families may be related to modernization and its attendant increase in individualism, as joint families are found less frequently in urban areas compared with rural areas. Conversely, the percentage of nuclear families is higher in urban areas, as is the percentage of single-parent families. Consistent with the modernization thesis is the finding that preference for family structure is related to the level of education of the family head. Families with the most educated heads are the least likely to be joint families and the most likely to be nuclear families compared with families having the least educated heads. Among the most educated the majority of families are nuclear families. In this context it can be argued that education, especially where it stresses Western values, is strongly associated with the nuclear family system and militates against the traditional extended family household.

China is another country where extended family living is more prevalent than it is in the West, despite all the changes of recent decades. The most distinctive feature of Chinese family structure concerns the preference for elderly people to live with one of their children. The living arrangement of one couple only, without co-residing children, is much less popular among elderly persons in China than it is in Western countries. Here, a large majority of elderly men and women live with their children. Elderly women are more likely to live with their children than elderly men, because elderly women are more likely to be widowed and economically dependent. They are also more likely to be asked by their children to co-reside in order to take care of grandchildren while the mothers go out to work. As a result, many more Chinese live in households of three or more generations than, for example, Americans do (Yi, 2002). Approximately one-quarter of the Chinese population live in households of three or more generations.

Living in extended family households responds to the needs of both the older generation and the younger generation. A newly married couple, for example, may move in with their parents until they can find accommodation of their own. Subsequently, when they have children, they may prefer to have a mother living with them to provide childcare. And later in life, when their parents are old and infirm, co-residence may be preferred in order that the elderly parents can more effectively receive care.

Evidence in support of this two-sided view of the benefits of extended family living comes from a study by Feinian Chen (Chen, 2005). On one hand, Chen found that the birth of children increases the odds of a couple having parents living with them. This suggests that co-residence with parents responds to the childcare needs of the adult children. Grandparents, and in particular paternal grandparents, often play an important role as childcare givers in China. On the other hand, widowhood makes it more likely that the surviving parent will live together with a child and his or her family. In addition to marital status, the health status of parents makes a difference to the chances of co-residence. If at least one of the parents is in need of help with daily living, then it is more likely that they will live with one of their children. Again, it seems that parental needs prompt parents to move in with their children. In sum, the evidence suggests that co-residence between the generations responds to both children's and parents' needs. It responds to children's needs early on (e.g. childcare needs) and later on it responds to parents' needs (e.g. health declines and widowhood). It appears that the persistence of extended family households in China is not only a reflection of the continuing influence of cultural traditions. In contemporary China, extended family living arrangements serve as an adaptive family strategy that helps family members cope with the requirements of daily life.

Historically, the type of extended family household favoured in Chinese culture has been the stem family, consisting of an elderly couple, and a married son and his wife and children. The stem family is a patrilineal intergenerational group in which a succession of males live together with their wives and dependent children, all sharing one household. There is still evidence of stem family preference today. While a significant minority of elderly people residing in three-generation households live with an adult daughter, a large majority of them live with an adult son (Yi, 2002). Parents who live with an adult child continue to be more likely to live with a son than with a daughter. However, it is likely that the preference for stem family living is declining slowly with modernization. Stem extended family households are less prevalent in towns and cities than they are in rural areas. Interestingly, the urban elderly are much more likely to live with daughters than the rural elderly are. The traditional idea of relying on sons for care in old age is much less popular in urban areas than it continues to be in rural areas, and it appears to be changing with modernization and urbanization. More and more old people in urban areas accept or even prefer to live with a daughter, perhaps because daughters are seen as more likely to provide better care to elderly parents than sons are.

Although preference for extended family living continues to be relatively high in East Asia, especially in China, change has clearly been occurring. One society where we can see major evidence of change is South Korea. When viewed cross-culturally, the number of Korean elderly living in extended family households is large, and in particular the number of elderly living with the eldest son's family is relatively high. The cultural ideal of the stem family continues to have an influence in Korea. However, extended family living has declined sharply in recent decades, and the biggest change has been in the number of elderly-only households. More older people are living independently, either with a spouse or on their own. This is mainly due to a very high rate of population mobility during the last four decades (Sung, 2001). Many Koreans have moved from rural areas to urban areas, and this movement has been higher among the young than among the old. This movement has left many elderly people in rural areas living on their own. Contrary to the popular image of rural areas as strongholds of tradition, in fact there are fewer elderly persons living with adult children in rural areas than in urban areas. The traditional norm dictating stem family co-residence, especially with the first son, has therefore been greatly weakened, especially in rural areas. There has been a significant decrease in the proportion of the elderly who live with the eldest son's family. Today, less than half of the elderly population co-resides with younger family members (Sug-In, 1998).

Despite the significant changes in recent decades, intergenerational co-residence continues to be practised by many families in Korea. This is largely a result of the continued importance of the value of filial piety. In the Korean cultural context, filial piety remains the most important value governing the younger generation's attitudes and behaviours towards parents. It is reinforced by public policy, and also by the mass media and educational channels in which exemplary performances are widely publicized in the form of news documentaries, reading materials, plays and literary works. The moral ideal underlying the practice of filial piety is that elderly people should be respected and cared for because of the sacrifices they made in order to raise the next generation. It is therefore felt that it is only right that when parents are at the age when they can no longer take care of themselves, they should be cared for by those whom they have raised.

Intergenerational co-residence occurs not only for normative reasons but also for practical reasons, reflecting the different needs of the different generations. Elderly parents often need practical assistance with the needs of daily living as well as economic support due to the existence of insufficient welfare programmes. It is therefore not surprising that age of parents and marital status are both factors affecting extended family living. The older parents are, the more likely they are to co-reside with younger family members. That is because they have greater difficulty looking after themselves and because they are more likely to have exhausted their financial resources. Marital status of elderly parents is also a factor affecting intergenerational co-residence because while parents tend to live separately from their children when both spouses are alive, when they are on their own parents tend to live with their adult children. Age and marital status are, of course, related since the older the parents are, the less likely it is that both parents will still be alive.

Intergenerational co-residence can also benefit the adult children as well as the parents. High housing prices make it very difficult for newly married couples to be independent, and the shortage of reliable and affordable childcare facilities encourages many working mothers to turn to their parents for assistance. The employment status of daughters-in-law therefore affects their preference for co-residence with parents, with employed daughters-in-law being more likely than non-employed daughters-in-law to prefer co-residence.

A fourth East Asian society in which the incidence of intergenerational co-residence continues to be relatively high is Japan, although change in family living arrangements appears to have occurred faster there than in China. Extended family households in Japan are generally interpreted as an expression of the belief in traditional cultural norms that emphasize filial duty and responsibility. Traditional norms favour co-residence between elderly parents and their adult children, and these norms continue to have some influence today. Intergenerational co-residence is legitimated and reinforced by the cultural ideal of the three-generation stem family, where elderly parents live with their eldest son and his family. However, the social context has undoubtedly changed. The prevalence of extended family households has declined substantially in recent decades, and it seems that norms of filial piety have weakened over time. In 1960, 86.8 per cent of people aged 65 and older lived with their children (Yamato, 2006). After the 1960s, however, the number of elderly people living with their children fell, while those living in elderly couple households and those living alone rose. By 2000, the number of elderly people living with their children had dropped to 49.5 per cent (29.4 per cent with married children, and 20.1 per cent with unmarried children), while more than 30 per cent lived in elderly couple households and 14.5 per cent lived alone. Nevertheless, extended family living continues to be higher in Japan than it is in the West.

Emiko Takagi and Merril Silverstein have hypothesized that, as the influence of traditional cultural norms has declined, people tend to engage in extended family living mainly for instrumental reasons (Takagi and Silverstein, 2006). It is the practical benefits of co-residence that explain the preference for extended family households, rather than a sense of social obligation. Therefore, family adaptive strategies should be common reasons for forming multigenerational households in Japan today. This does not mean that traditional norms have entirely disappeared. Rather, norms of filial piety and instrumental calculations interact in complex ways.

Takagi and Silverstein have found that traditional norms about intergenerational co-residence enhance the possibility of living in a stem family household. Consistent with the cultural preference for the stem family, households that consist of married children and their parents are primarily those in which sons and daughters-in-law reside. At the same time, a substantial number of elderly parents in Japan still express a desire for traditional living arrangements yet are unable to realize them in practice. Clearly, factors other than traditional norms also enter into decisions about whether the different generations should actually live together. Emiko Takagi and Merril Silverstein also found, then, that extended family living tends to be adopted only when there is some need for it, and the means exist to meet that need. Household extension in Japan is found to be related to the needs and resources of parents. For example, being widowed means that the individual has lost someone with whom to share the tasks of daily living, particularly for men, and it may lead to a loss of income, particularly for women. Widowhood entails greater unmet needs and it is therefore associated with intergenerational co-residence. Likewise, being in poor health increases the need for assistance and it too is associated with living in an extended family household. At the same time as parents have needs that adult children can meet by living with them, some parents have resources that make intergenerational co-residence attractive to the children as well. Thus, parents who own their own homes are also more likely to co-reside with their adult children, because they can meet the child's need for housing. However, this pattern of co-residence tends to differ from the traditional stem family. It is mainly unmarried sons and daughters who co-reside with their parents for this reason. Evidently, family adaptive strategies are significant factors in household extension in Japan today.

Japan is not the only society in which intergenerational co-residence is an adaptive strategy to help meet family members' needs of daily living. Despite a general cultural preference for residential autonomy between the generations, extended family living for instrumental reasons can also be found in Western societies. Patricia Ahmed and Rebecca Emigh, for example, have studied household composition in Eastern Europe in these terms (Ahmed and Emigh, 2005). They argue that extended family households in that part of the world are a response to such conditions as poverty, kinship responsibilities and the labour requirements of agriculture. Ahmed and Emigh tested their hypotheses in a survey of households in Bulgaria, Hungary, Poland, Romania and Russia, and found they were confirmed. The poor, for example, are more likely to live in extended family households, because this enables them to pool their resources and helps them to cope with resource scarcity. For similar reasons, single motherhood is associated with household extension in all of the countries. Single mothers frequently have low incomes, and sharing resources with a family member helps them to cope with the economic disadvantages of their marital status. Also, living in the same household as a parent or a sibling facilitates family childcare when the mother must go out to work. Responsibilities for elderly kin are also related to the practice of household extension. There is some evidence to suggest that the retired are more likely to live in extended family households, despite the fact that they prefer living on their own. Finally, Patricia Ahmed and Rebecca Emigh found that households which cultivate agricultural holdings are more likely to be extended. In such cases, living in extended family households helps the family members to pool their labour so that their agricultural activity can be more productive. Economic disadvantage, care for the elderly, and agricultural productivity are all related to household extension in Eastern Europe.

The idea that extended family households often function as safety nets for economically disadvantaged people has also been important in family studies in the United States. Yoshinori Kamo, for example, reports that household extension is related to the availability of economic resources (Kamo, 2000). The larger the personal income of the individual, the smaller is the likelihood of living in an extended family household. This suggests that individuals prefer to live independently when they are financially able to do so, but that they will live in extended family households when economic resources are scarce. Anne Pebley and Laura Rudkin report that young adults who remain in their parents' home generally do so because they are less able to live independently (Pebley and Rudkin, 1999). Poor labour market conditions and higher parental incomes cause adult children to leave home at later ages. Pebley and Rudkin also report that adult children who move back in with their parents often do so because they are in transition from one established role to another, such as experiencing separation from a spouse. Marital disruption is in fact an important cause of co-residence in three-generation households in which adult children and their children live in their (grand)parents' household. Grandparents are more likely to provide a home for adult children and grandchildren following the divorce of the adult children if they live nearby and have a close relationship with the custodial parent.

Another issue in the United States has been the existence of differences in household extension practices between racial/ethnic groups. African-Americans, Hispanics and Asians form extended family households more often than non-Hispanic whites. Whether these differences exist because of different cultural traditions or for socioeconomic reasons needs to be clarified. Yoshinori Kamo has examined this issue using a classification of three types of extended families (Kamo, 2000). First, there are upwardly extended households. These occur when the head of the household lives with anyone in the previous generation, such as an elderly parent. Second, downwardly extended households are those in which the head of the household lives with an adult child or grandchild.

And third, horizontally extended households exist when the head of household lives with anyone in the same generation other than his or her spouse. Different racial/ethnic groups show different preferences for these three types of extended family households. Downward extension is disproportionately common among African-Americans (and among Hispanic Americans to a lesser extent). For example, African-American grandchildren are more likely than children of other ethnic groups to live with their grandparents (Pebley and Rudkin, 1999). Upward extension is common among Asians. And horizontal extension is common among Hispanics (and among Asians and African-Americans to a lesser extent). Non-Hispanic Whites are much less likely than other groups to form extended family households of any type.

It seems likely that downward household extension is more common among African-Americans than it is among other racial/ethnic groups largely due to the substantial proportions of teenage pregnancies and single mothers among African-Americans, and the strong traditions of assistance from African-American mothers for their children and grandchildren. Black grandmothers historically have played a more important role in child-rearing than white grandparents. Reliance upon grandmothers among African-Americans may be partly a reflection of particular social norms, as well as practical adaptations to higher rates of poverty and relatively poor job prospects among young adults. Asian-Americans, on the other hand, are prone to live in intergenerational households due to their cultural traditions of filial responsibility of adult children for aged parents. Horizontal extension may be more common among Hispanic Americans as a result of values of familism that place commitment to the collectivity above the individual, and because of the large numbers of recent migrants for whom living with a sibling is an adaptive strategy for adjustment to living in a new country.

It is worth noting that Yoshinori Kamo finds that the differences between household extension practices of racial/ethnic groups persist even when predictors of extended family living, such as income and single parenthood, are controlled. African-American single mothers are more likely to live with their parents than are their counterparts in other racial/ethnic groups, even after controlling for economic and demographic variables that predict extended family living. Similarly, elderly Asians remain more likely to live with their adult children after household extension predictors are controlled. And foreign-born Hispanics are more likely to live with their siblings net of economic and demographic factors. All these findings suggest that there are cultural variations within the American population, in addition to the influence of family adaptive strategies. While Americans of all racial/ethnic groups form extended family households for instrumental reasons, some of them also do it for cultural reasons according to their particular traditions.

KIN SUPPORT

Forming extended family households is one means of providing support to kin in need of help, but it is not the only one. There is also financial support in the form of money or gifts, emotional support, and practical support in the form of assistance with the tasks of daily living. All these forms of support can be exchanged between people who do not live together, and they often are.

Support between non-co-resident kin does not necessarily follow the same pattern as co-residence. For example, whereas African-American single mothers are more likely to live with their parents than are white single mothers, fewer African-American single mothers receive parental assistance of any kind than white single mothers do (Aldous, 1995). Several nationally representative studies in the United States have found that Whites see more of kin and exchange more assistance than do African-Americans (Johnson, 2000). It is likely that this pattern is a reflection of the differential availability of resources. Visiting relatives and entertaining relatives requires financial resources, which are generally scarcer among African-Americans than among Whites. Also, African-Americans have lower rates of economic exchange between generations than Whites because they have fewer resources and hence less to give.

Natalia Sarkisian and Naomi Gerstel report that both African-American and white survey respondents engage in the giving and receiving of support, but the patterns of support vary (Sarkisian and Gerstel, 2004). Whites are more likely than African-Americans to be involved in transfers of financial support. Because Whites are more likely to have higher socioeconomic status than African-Americans, they are more likely to have the resources necessary to give kin money. On the other hand, African-Americans are more likely than Whites to engage in the giving and receiving of practical support, including transportation help, household help, and childcare. Racial differences among women are greater than racial differences among men. Across race, men are very similar, though African-American men are less likely to give, receive or exchange financial resources than Whites. Women exhibit the same pattern of racial differences in financial support as men, but in addition they show differences in practical support. In particular, African-American women are significantly more likely than white women to engage in balanced reciprocal exchanges of transportation help, household help, and childcare. Sarkisian and Gerstel's data show that African-Americans and Whites have different patterns of kin support, and these differences are attributable to cultural values, nuclear and extended family composition, gender, and socioeconomic position.

Socioeconomic position is a general factor influencing the giving and receiving of support. For example, studies in the United States show that transfers of money from parents to adult children are associated with higher income and higher socioeconomic status. This is also visible in a study of intergenerational exchanges between older parents and their adult children in Britain (Grundy, 2005). Emily Grundy examined the relationship between giving support and housing tenure, which is an indicator of socioeconomic status. She found that the proportion of parents providing help for a child was slightly higher among home owners than among tenants. Parental income was positively associated with provision of help with money, and tenants had lower odds, in comparison with home owners, of providing either financial help or other help. On the other hand, parents who were tenants rather than home owners included a higher proportion of individuals who received help from a child. Thus better-off home owners were more likely to be helping their children, not only with money but in other ways as well, and were less likely to receive help from children.

The amount of resources that parents possess influences the extent to which they receive help from their children. Generally, the fewer resources that parents have, the more likely they are to be given help. For example, it was found in a study of support given to older parents in Taiwan that adult children are more likely to provide financial support for parents who are not working and who have low incomes than they are to help parents who are better off (Lin *et al.*, 2003). Another factor that influences flows of support, in addition to the extent of the economic resources of parents, is how many children the parents have. Lin *et al.* (2003) report from their study in Taiwan that parents who had only one child were only half as likely to receive any help as parents with more than one adult child in the family. Among the different types of support, this was especially so for financial support, which was most likely to be shared among siblings.

In families with more than one child, it can make a difference which child provides support and what the type of support is. Overall, the study of intergenerational support in Taiwan found that sons are almost twice as likely as daughters to provide help, reflecting the cultural preference for help from male children in that country. Sons are expected to assume the major responsibility for taking care of their parents in that country. However, the relationship between gender of adult children and level of support for older parents varies according to the type of support provided. Sons are much more likely than daughters to provide financial support, presumably due in part to the greater financial resources possessed by men, and sons are somewhat more likely to provide help with instrumental activities such as shopping, meal preparation, transportation and managing finances. On the other hand, both sons and daughters are about as likely to provide help with activities of daily living such as bathing, dressing, and maintaining toilet functions. However, gender can make a difference. Sons are more likely to provide assistance with activities of daily living for their fathers than for their mothers, but the parent's gender is unrelated to the likelihood of daughters providing intimate care. Daughters in Taiwan are slightly more likely than sons to provide material support for older parents in the form of food, clothing and other goods. Probably most of this support takes the form of providing food, reflecting the gender division of labour in household tasks.

Having children is one important way of gaining access to support in later life, for those who need it. So, too, is marriage. People who are married are generally seen as being less in need of other supports than those who are not married, because they have a spouse who can help them. In Taiwan, for example, daughters are less likely to provide assistance with activities of daily living or instrumental activities, or to give financial support, to parents who live with a spouse compared with parents who do not have a spouse present in the household. Children are important substitute sources of support for older parents who are not married.

Marriage is a source of support in its own right, but it also links the individual to other persons such as children and the relatives of the marriage partner. Not surprisingly, therefore, people who are married differ from those who have never been married in the main source of social support. Married people depend more on kin for support, whereas never married people depend more on friends. The effect of being married on reliance upon kin for support increases with the number of years that a person has been married (Curran, McLanahan and Knab, 2003). Presumably, with increased contact with kin over time, people have the opportunity to develop more extensive exchange relationships.

Since marital status is related to source of support, it is also to be expected that marital disruption will have an effect on support from kin. This expectation is confirmed in a study of social support among the elderly in the United States conducted by Sara Curran, Sara McLanahan and Jean Knab (Curran, McLanahan and Knab, 2003). They found that the odds of perceiving support from kin are lower for people who have experienced a marital disruption compared with those who are currently married. Interestingly, the effect of marital disruption was stronger for people who are divorced than for people who are widowed.

Loss of a partner affects not only access to kin, but also the extent of need for support and the resources available to help others. Widowhood therefore has an impact upon exchanges of support with kin, especially adult children. The usual pattern of social exchange between the generations is that parents give more to children than children give to parents, except when the parents are very old. Customary patterns of exchange may be changed, however, when a life-altering event such as widowhood occurs. Loss of a partner may mean loss of financial resources, especially for women, and this is likely to increase the widowed person's need for financial support. At the same time they have fewer resources with which to provide support to others. Also, with loss of a partner there may be a greater need for assistance with practical tasks of daily living. If the married couple had a division of labour in which each partner depended upon the other to do things for them, then the loss of a partner may create a gap in their lives which they look to others to fill. Consequently, bereaved spouses who are coping with the challenges of adjusting to the loss of a partner may become more dependent upon their children, and less able to provide support for them.

Reliance upon a spouse who has died may be an especial problem for current cohorts of the elderly, due to the fact that most of them have followed a traditional division of labour between the spouses throughout their married lives. Most women who are elderly today devoted more time and effort to their families than they did to earning an income and acquiring financial resources for their old age. They therefore depend heavily upon their husbands for their economic well-being when they are old. They are also used to relying upon their husbands for financial management and decision-making. At the same time, elderly men have usually been accustomed to occupying the role of breadwinner, as a result of which they have left responsibility for nurturing their children and providing emotional support to their wives. This traditional division of labour is likely to create differences between older men and women as they adjust to widowhood. Those who are bereaved may depend on their children for assistance with tasks customarily performed by members of the opposite sex. At the same time, adult children may not receive the same kinds of help from a widowed parent as they did when both parents were alive, because of the different skills and resources possessed by each parent.

Jung-Hwa Ha, Deborah Carr, Rebecca Utz and Randolph Nesse have examined these issues in a study of the elderly in Detroit, USA (Ha *et al.*, 2006). They report that widowhood has a large and significant effect on the surviving parent's overall dependence on his or her children. Widowed persons have levels of dependence upon their children that are higher than those who are still married. At the same time, widowhood decreases children's dependence upon their parents. Widowed parents are more reliant on their children than are married parents, and they provide less support for their children.

Concerning gender differences, Ha *et al.* found that widows report significantly higher levels of dependence on their children for financial and legal advice, and for errands and other chores, than widowers do. On the other hand, widowed mothers report higher levels of dependence of their children upon them for emotional and instrumental support than do widowed fathers. Clearly, patterns of parent–child dependence differ by gender. It seems that widows seek more help in managing financial and legal matters because they do not possess the skills or experience to deal with these matters, which were presumably the responsibility of their late husbands. However, it also appears that they are more effective than widowers in providing emotional and instrumental support since they are accustomed to taking care of other family members. Intergenerational relations reflect different skills and dependencies in the older generation that develop as a result of the gender division of labour. Parents tend to turn to their children for those gendered resources and skills that they lack, and they provide assistance for their children in those areas where they are best able to help.

The extent of kin support may also be influenced by the larger institutional structure within which families are located. This is the conclusion drawn by Reiko Yamato about changing attitudes towards dependence of elderly parents upon their children in postwar Japan (Yamato, 2006). She hypothesizes that the perceived needs of elderly parents for support are affected by the availability of public welfare programmes such as pensions and care services. When such welfare provisions become sufficiently reliable, then they will affect people's attitudes towards elderly dependence on children. Certainly, attitudes towards the financial dependence of elderly parents upon their children have been changing in Japan. More and more Japanese people see elderly dependence on children as less desirable, even though the country has a cultural tradition of familism and filial piety. Until the mid-1960s, Japanese elderly people took for granted financial dependence on children in old age, which they saw as an economic necessity. People's attitudes towards financial dependence of the elderly upon their children began to change, however, from the late 1960s. Initially, this seems to have been due to changes in the economy. The shift from an agricultural to an industrial economy, and the growth of employment in corporations, meant that economic provision changed from self-employment and the availability of family property to one based on paid employment. The elderly could therefore no longer assume that they could depend economically upon their eldest son in return for the inheritance of a family business. Change continued in the 1980s with improvement of the employee's pension benefit scheme, when the pension benefits came to provide basic subsistence for a large number of elderly people without their needing financial support from their children. Financial dependence on the public pension system has become the norm in contemporary Japan. Today, a substantial majority of Japanese elderly people think they would rely on pension benefits for livelihood in old age, and those who would rely financially upon their children have become relatively rare.

DISCUSSION

In this chapter we have seen that flows of support between kin continue to be important, even in Western societies that have experienced the greatest effects of modernization. In the modern Western societies, kinship ties tend to take the form of the modified extended family. Co-residence between adults other than spouses is rare, but extended family members continue to maintain social ties and to help each other in various ways. In particular, ties are maintained between parents and their adult children. Patterns of support vary between racial groups.

Outside Western societies, co-residence between adults other than spouses is more common. This is notably the case in East Asia, of which four societies were discussed here. Extended family households were examined in India, China, South Korea and Japan, and local influences on co-residence were described. In China and Japan, the ideal of the stem family household continues to be important, though changes are occurring most notably in Japan.

Finally, we considered kin support other than co-residence and discussed its relationship to social stratification and institutional change. Race and class are both factors affecting the giving and receiving of support, which are interconnected in interesting ways.

Social support between kin, especially parents and children, is a topic that has become increasingly important in social policy analyses in recent years. This is partly related to population ageing, as a result of which there is increased interest in the extent to which older people will require assistance from kin or from the state. Kin and the state are to some extent alternative providers of support, as we saw in the discussion of changing attitudes towards financial dependence of elderly parents in Japan upon their children. Which alternative is chosen has implications for state policies.

13 Family and state

Family life occurs in the private sphere of modern societies, but it is not a purely private matter. Family issues are discussed in the mass media, and arguments are proposed for and against different family practices and outcomes. As a result, interests develop in regulating family life, and governments adopt policies towards families which are formulated into laws affecting family life. Laws regulate such matters as who can marry whom, the responsibilities of family members towards one another, and the benefits, supports and controls that the state provides for families of different types. The state often adopts a role as intervener in family life, either to meet family needs or for social control over families that are judged to be failing to meet their responsibilities.

Governments everywhere have policies that are designed to help families meet their needs of daily living. However, their involvement in family life varies between different countries, reflecting different cultural traditions and political priorities. In social-democratic states the aim of the state is to promote social equality, including equality within families and between families of different types. Such states are typically interested in promoting gender equality, for example by encouraging the employment of women with children. Also, social-democratic states provide extensive income transfers and other supports in the form of universal programmes that provide the same benefits for every citizen. A wide range of services are universally available as entitlements of citizens. In contrast, government policies in corporatist welfare states are not directed at social equality so much as they are directed at family stability. There is a preference for retaining traditional family forms which are believed to work well, and social groups that support family life are encouraged. Finally, liberal welfare states tend not to adopt formal family policies of any kind unless induced to do so by pressures to solve social problems or in order to support the market economy. Here, explicit state involvement in family life is limited, and expenditures on families tend to be low in order to keep taxes down. Income support measures are therefore less extensive than they are in social-democratic states, and they tend to take the form of targeted programmes which help a small number of people in greatest need. A limited set of services are provided that are directed towards specifically defined target groups.

THE SOCIAL-DEMOCRATIC STATE

The Scandinavian countries, in particular Sweden, are the classic examples of social-democratic states. Here, the state has been actively involved in developing social programmes that are intended to alleviate social inequalities and other social problems. Beginning in the 1970s, family policy in the Scandinavian countries witnessed steady growth, in terms of both the range of family issues for which policies were formulated and the levels of state expenditures. For example, legislation was enacted that expanded entitlements to maternity, paternity and parental leave. Through these policies the state supported employed parents' care for their offspring by guaranteeing entitlements to leave of absence at times of family need. Employed parents were given the opportunity to care for young children, while retaining job security and enjoying wage compensation. Also, high-quality, state-sponsored childcare was provided so that working parents could feel confident that their children were being well looked after. Making high-quality childcare available was regarded as a political priority and as part of the commitment of the welfare state to its citizens (Leira, 1993). Extensive public investments were made in the education and care of pre-school children, which both supported women's work outside the home and became an avenue for the employment of women.

The Scandinavian welfare state of the 1970s and 1980s helped to create a family form in which both women and men work for pay while their children are looked after in publicly supported day care. In addition to providing day care, the expanded welfare state became a major employer of women and hence promoted mothers' employment indirectly. In the welfare state, jobs were developed in areas commonly identified as preferable to women, namely in education, health and social welfare, as well as in public administration.

Up to the 1990s, the development of family policy was an integral part of the expansion of the Scandinavian welfare state. Beginning in the 1990s, however, the Scandinavian economies ran into difficulties which were reflected in financial and political pressures to reduce the reach of the welfare state. These pressures were felt most intensely in Sweden and

Finland. All areas of social policy experienced cuts, due to large budget deficits and problems in raising loans to provide benefits for the growing numbers of unemployed. The cuts included changes to family policy. Reductions were made to benefits for families with children because the number of recipients and the corresponding expenditure on benefits were high (Hiilamo, 2004). These cuts were largely reversed in Sweden in the early 2000s, but in Finland that was not the case. For Sweden, the depression of the 1990s proved to be a temporary period of retrenchment which was followed by intensive development of family policy in the early 2000s, whereas in Finland the cuts were more long-lasting. Public provision of day care has remained high and was even expanded during the 1990s, at a time of austerity when cutbacks were implemented in many other areas of social support.

Overall, support for family policy has remained high in Finland and Sweden, and the cuts made during the depression of the 1990s did not lead to profound changes in the family policy systems of either country. By comparison with other countries, both Finland and Sweden still offer day care at low cost on a universal basis, parental benefits include a long period of leave with compensation at a high level, and cash child benefits are above the average level. Sweden and Finland therefore continue to follow the social-democratic model, and their welfare states have retained their structural features, although they have become less generous. In particular, the principle of universalism was strengthened in both countries, largely due to the replacement of tax deductions by cash child benefits in Finland, and to the increase in cash child benefits in Sweden. Also, the expansion in day care strengthened the service aspect of family policy in both countries, in a manner that added to the universalism of the welfare state.

THE CORPORATIST STATE

Germany is a good example of a corporatist welfare state. Here, citizens are guaranteed a basic economic minimum and have access to essential health and social services, but this is done in such a way that it does not disturb the preference for traditional family forms. For example, social policies provide differentiated access to economic resources based on marital status. Among women with children, married women have on average the best access, followed by divorced women, with unmarried mothers having the least favourable position. Single mothers receive financial benefits from the state but they have lower incomes than married mothers on average, and they must work longer hours than married mothers because they do not have a husband's income upon which to depend. As a result, single mothers tend to be pitied because they are poor and overworked (Klett-Davies, 1997).

German family policy also tends to encourage families in which mothers stay at home to care for their children. There are strong incentives that favour breadwinner–homemaker families where one parent has less attachment to the labour market than the other. Law and policy are specifically formulated to encourage child-rearing to take place in the home, with one of the parents focusing on child-rearing and family responsibilities (Trzcinski, 2000). Family policy in Germany is based on the premise that young children are provided with the best opportunities for human development when they are primarily cared for by a parent in their own home. As a result, German parents are more likely than parents in a country like Sweden to divide their labour, with one parent going out to work full-time and the other parent staying at home or working only part-time. This pattern is changing, as female employment has increased in Germany in recent years. Nevertheless, many German women still do not work a full week or they are not employed at all, especially when they have young children.

THE LIBERAL STATE

The United States and Britain are examples of liberal states. Social policies in these countries tend to be directed at targeted groups and aimed at improving the workings of the market economy. In the United States, in particular, dependency upon the state is discouraged, and it is preferred that families should draw upon their own resources through their participation in the labour market. For example, there has been much concern in the United States about the degree of dependence of single mothers upon support from the state. Welfare support for families headed by single mothers became a major concern in the 1990s. As a result, reforms to welfare were introduced in 1996 that were intended to get more single mothers off welfare and employed in the labour force.

Welfare reforms have reduced cash assistance and have enforced a higher labour force participation rate. The outcome is that fewer single mothers are now relying exclusively upon cash assistance. In that sense the reforms have been successful in reducing dependence upon the state, although many single mothers who leave welfare still depend upon other state benefits such as Medicaid or Food Stamps. The reforms appear to have been less successful in improving the economic circumstances of families headed by single mothers, since many employed single mothers who left welfare earn low incomes (Ezawa and Fujiwara, 2005). The majority of single mothers who leave welfare are in work, but they often experience unstable employment and they tend to be employed in low wage jobs. Even though work participation rates have increased among single mothers and they have become less dependent upon cash assistance, one of the consequences has been to increase the numbers of the working poor who still need state benefits in order to survive. Maintenance of a strong safety net is therefore crucial for the welfare of single mothers and their children even when the mothers are employed. Public policies which support the working poor are important to single mothers' economic independence despite low incomes.

In Britain, one targeted group for social policy in recent years has been children (Featherstone, 2006; Lister, 2006). State expenditures on financial support for children and on childcare/early years services have increased significantly. Children are regarded as good investments because healthy and well-educated children will become successful and productive adults. Investing in children is regarded as an investment in the future. That is because children who are able to realize their full potential will be able to take advantage of life's opportunities. People's security is thought not to come from the state but from their capacity to use the changing opportunities open to them. Thus, the emphasis is on the state investing in human capital. In this policy discourse, social and economic concerns are linked, and the integration of people into the market economy is encouraged.

The contemporary British state is keen on preparing its citizens to adapt to global economic change so as to enhance the competitiveness of the labour force under new economic conditions. The modern economy is based on the possession of knowledge and skills, and therefore it is perceived to be the business of government to ensure that people have the education, skills and personal qualities that will make them successful in the labour market. In the policies of New Labour this means, among other things, targeting the resources of the state on the reduction of child poverty. Policies targeted on child poverty are less concerned with overall goals of social equality than they are with human potential and productivity. That is because the emphasis in the British welfare state is less upon income maintenance and the consumption needs of families, and more upon investing in people's abilities and thereby enhancing their capacity to participate in the productive economy. In this context, poor children are believed to suffer from disadvantages that hamper their adaptability and limit their economic success. Poor children are thought to suffer from disadvantages such as less stimulating home environments and early school leaving, and reducing child poverty will therefore help to increase the extent of human development in the British population. In this way public policy reduces the probability of future costs of school failure and crime, and fosters employability.

THE FAMILY AS A SOLUTION TO
SOCIAL PROBLEMS

Public policy makers do not only seek to find ways of supporting families in order to improve family outcomes, but they also use the family as an instrument for policies to solve social problems. For example, population ageing has led to increased concern about the relative contributions of families and the state to the provision of support for the elderly. It is feared that if families do not assume a larger role in support of the elderly then the latter will become an increasing burden on the state, leading to a dramatic increase in rates of taxation and the diversion of resources from other purposes. As a result, the Japanese government has recently tried to shift some of the cost of the social security system back onto families (Elmelech, 2005). Nationwide efforts have been made to preserve the traditional values associated with care for the elderly.

In Britain there has been great concern in recent years about crime and anti-social behaviour more generally among children, and this has been reflected in policies to require parents to take more responsibility for their children. Under the Crime and Disorder Act (1998) and the Anti-Social Behaviour Act (2003) compulsory Parenting Orders can be obtained to ensure that parents control their children's behaviour, and child curfews can be imposed that parents are expected to enforce (Lister, 2006). Also, parents can be fined, or even jailed, if their children engage in persistent truancy from school. All of these measures are designed to make parents exercise greater control over their children, so that they will grow up to be responsible, law-abiding and productive citizens. In these ways state policy in Britain today places a renewed emphasis on parenting and the responsibilities of parents as solutions to social problems. In the process, it places a great deal of faith in parents' ability to control the behaviour of their children as they grow older.

In Scotland, the Anti-social Behaviour etc. (Scotland) Act of 2004 has extended Anti-social Behaviour Orders to children, while parents can be subject to Parenting Orders which require parents to comply with specified requirements, including attendance at parental counselling or guidance sessions (Cleland and Tisdall, 2005; Tisdall, 2006). The extension of Anti-social Behaviour Orders to children reflects concern that anti-social acts among children are precursors of adult anti-social behaviour. As a result, there is considerable interest in children's developmental careers in relation to anti-social behaviour. Anti-social Behaviour Orders are considered to be a form of early intervention and prevention. An Anti-social Behaviour Order is intended to stop young people from persistent offending and encourage them to avoid a future career in crime. Factors deemed to cause anti-social behaviour in children, such as low parental involvement and poor parental supervision, are therefore a focus of attention. The trigger for an application for a Parenting Order is thus the child's anti-social behaviour or criminal conduct, and the perceived need to stop such behaviour or conduct. A Parenting Order is aimed specifically at getting a parent to control and change the child's behaviour or conduct. The underlying assumption here is that parents have the responsibility for controlling their children. Responsibility for the child's actions is held to lie with the parents, rather than recognizing children's responsibility for their own actions. According to Cleland and Tisdall, Parenting Orders have changed the relationship between the parent and the state, holding parents accountable to the community for their children's behaviour in a new way (Cleland and Tisdall, 2005). In this new relationship the courts take on an increasing role in state intervention in the lives of children and their parents.

In the United States, state intervention in family life includes promoting marriage as a solution to societal ills. The main concern has been with the costs of supporting unmarried mothers and their children on welfare, because they lack the income of a husband to support them. Expanding welfare rolls from the 1960s on motivated a concern to reduce welfare dependency. At a time of family change, including higher divorce rates and increased numbers of births outside wedlock, one of the causes of greater dependence on welfare was perceived to be the collapse of marriage. Steps to correct this situation were taken in 1996 with the Personal Responsibility and Work Opportunity Reconciliation Act (PRWORA). The thrust of PRWORA is to alleviate government responsibility for the poor by privatizing it through the mechanism of the family. PRWORA explicitly listed the formation and maintenance of two-parent families as one of its primary goals, and it permitted states to utilize federal funds to promote marriage among welfare recipients (Onwuachi-Willig, 2005). Through the Personal Responsibility and Work Opportunity Reconciliation Act, the US Congress intended to help end the dependence of needy parents on government benefits by encouraging welfare recipients to marry. In doing this, Congress was acting on the assumption that marriage, and a husband's income, would remedy women and children's reliance on public benefits. The American state is therefore involved in promoting heterosexual marriage as a way of reducing the burden of dependants upon the public purse.

LEGISLATING THE FAMILY

Heterosexual marriage is the preferred basis of family life in American public policy. As a result, Amy Lind argues that in the USA institutionalized heterosexuality plays an important role in shaping and influencing social welfare agendas (Lind, 2004). By 'institutionalized heterosexuality' she means the set of ideas, institutions and relationships that make the heterosexual family the societal norm, while making homosexual/queer families into abnormal or deviant families. In this process, the state plays a key role. Through legislation such as the Personal Responsibility and Work Opportunity Reconciliation Act, the state is involved in defining and promoting what a normal family should be like. The family of the American federal state in fact is based upon heterosexual marriage, and it excludes other family forms such as same-sex couples. This is most explicit in the Defense of Marriage Act (DOMA), also passed in 1996, which defines marriage as a legal union between a man and a woman. DOMA allows the states the right not to honour other states' marriage contracts where marriage is defined differently. It also paved the way for some states to pass their own versions of the Defense of Marriage Act. As a result, a state that has passed its own DOMA does not recognize domestic partnerships of same-sex couples that were married in a state where they are recognized. Together, the Defense of Marriage Act and the Personal Responsibility and Work Opportunity Reconciliation Act constitute a national policy context within which the normative family is legislated. In this way the state actively defines and shapes family forms in American society.

DISCUSSION

Altogether the state impinges on family life in three ways. First, the state provides services and supports for families that help them meet their needs of daily living. Second, the state exercises controls over families that are intended to reduce social problems. And third, state policies define, implicitly or explicitly, what counts as family, and they legislate the normative form of family life.

State services and supports are often conceptualized as a particular aspect of state functioning known as the welfare state. Welfare states are prominent social institutions in the modern world, but they do not take the same form everywhere. Three forms of the welfare state can be identified: the social-democratic state, the corporatist state, and the liberal state. In social-democratic states, such as those found in Scandinavia, the state provides extensive services and supports that are intended to reduce inequalities between families and within families. Between families, the state provides income support programmes that are intended to ameliorate class differences. Within families, the state provides programmes such as accessible and affordable childcare that are intended to reduce gender inequality by facilitating the employment of women. Corporatist states also provide services and supports for families, but they are usually less extensive than in social-democratic states and there is less emphasis on changing traditional family forms. In Germany, for instance, social policies continue to support families in which married mothers stay home with their children, and the level of employment among mothers is therefore lower than it is in a country such as Sweden. Liberal states such as Britain or the USA provide the least extensive services and supports for families, which target specific population groups. In contemporary Britain, for example, children are an important group that has become the target of new social policies.

In addition to supporting the functioning of families, states also seek to control families in the pursuit of public policy objectives. Certain families are perceived as creating specific kinds of social problems, and so the state attempts to reduce those problems by changing patterns of family life in some families. In contemporary Britain, for example, the courts can now pass Parenting Orders that are directed at the parents of children who have engaged in anti-social behaviour. Parenting Orders are intended to make these parents control their children's behaviour so that they do not offend members of the community. Also, we have seen that in the United States of America federal welfare legislation has been invoked to promote marriage among single mothers, in order to reduce their dependence upon government support payments.

Finally, state policies help to define the normative form of family life for a society. At the federal level in the USA this takes the form of defining heterosexual marriage as the normal basis for family life. In so doing, the state discriminates against same-sex couples who do not follow conventional patterns of sexuality.

14 Sexuality

Sexual relations are an important feature of family life. Couples, married or unmarried, engage in sex, though frequency declines with increasing age (Christopher and Sprecher, 2000; Ghuman, 2005). Sexual intercourse is more common in marriage, but it occurs outside marriage as well. Here, there has been a change in attitudes in recent decades. Attitudes towards premarital sex in particular have generally become more permissive over time. In the USA, for example, fewer respondents have rated sexual relations before marriage as 'always wrong', and more have rated them as 'not wrong at all', in recent, compared with earlier, years (Christopher and Sprecher, 2000). Predictors of sexual permissiveness in the United States include low religiosity, being politically liberal and being young, male and single.

Attitudes towards premarital sexuality have also become more tolerant in the Netherlands (Kraaykamp, 2002). Approval of sexual intercourse when people want to get married increased from only 21 per cent in 1965 to 83 per cent in 1991. Today most Dutch people condone sexual intercourse before marriage. Also, a majority of the population support the idea that a girl is allowed to have sex with a boy when she is in love with him. In 1970, less than half, 44 per cent of the population, agreed with this idea. By 1991 the number indicating their support for premarital sexual intercourse in a context of love had risen to 69 per cent. However, support for sexuality outside a love relationship has not changed as much, and it is still endorsed by only a small minority. Most people believe that an emotional bond between partners should exist before sexual relations are permitted to occur.

Predictors of sexual permissiveness in the Netherlands include educational attainment, low religiosity, young age, being single and being male. To begin with, more educated people are less likely to adhere to traditional values concerning moral issues than are less educated people. Consistent with this pattern, more highly educated individuals are significantly more likely to approve of sex before marriage than are the less educated. Religiosity is another significant factor in sexual permissiveness in the Netherlands, as it is in the USA, because most religions transmit restrictive moral standards with respect to sexuality. Not surprisingly, engagement in religion as indicated by church attendance is associated with less permissive attitudes towards premarital sexual relations. Age is also a factor affecting sexual permissiveness. Older people react more negatively to premarital sexuality than do younger people. Also, marital status is related to attitudes about premarital sexuality. Single people are more permissive than married, divorced or widowed persons. Finally, there is a gender difference in attitudes. Women are more conservative on matters of premarital sexual behaviour than are men.

The gender difference in attitudes towards premarital sexuality observed in the USA and the Netherlands seems to be quite general, as it is also reported to occur in Hai Duong Province, Vietnam (Ghuman, 2005). Within both rural and urban areas, women are significantly more likely than men to offer conservative views. Women in urban communities are less likely to disapprove of having sex with a future spouse than their rural counterparts, but nevertheless they are still more likely to disapprove of it than are men living in urban areas. In Vietnam, too, attitudes towards premarital sexuality appear to have been changing. More recent cohorts are significantly less likely than older cohorts to profess conservative views, though this relationship is more pronounced among men than among women. However, in Hai Duong Province, Vietnam, attitudes about premarital sex generally remain conservative. Most individuals in both rural and urban areas do not agree that sex and expressions of intimacy before marriage are permissible. Even among the most recent cohorts, 40 per cent of men and about 70 per cent of women still strongly disagree that having premarital sex with a future spouse is acceptable.

If premarital sexual relationships are contested terrain, the same is even more true of relationships in which men have sex with men and women have sex with women. These relationships are not endorsed by most religions, and they frequently encounter opposition. As a result, sexual relationships between people of the same sex cannot rely on the taken-for-granted assumptions of conventional society. This is the case, for example, with lesbian motherhood.

LESBIAN MOTHERHOOD

An increasing number of lesbians are choosing to raise children in the context of an openly lesbian lifestyle. However, this choice is not without its difficulties. According to Amy Hequembourg and Michael Farrell, lesbian mothers in America face problems of maintaining a dissonant identity (Hequembourg and Farrell, 1999). On the one hand motherhood is an identity that is highly valued by conventional society because it contributes to the maintenance of society. On the other hand being lesbian is an identity that is not conventionally supported and it is regarded in a negative way. As a result, lesbian mothers find that their identity as mothers is questioned, as many people doubt whether they can be good mothers. When lesbian mothers interact with members of their mainstream social networks, such as parents, teachers, co-workers, legal officials and medical providers, they must struggle to define their identity as a good mother. In particular, the threat of losing their children is often present for lesbian mothers who were once heterosexually married (Nations, 1997). Ex-husbands and other family members may challenge lesbian mothers as 'unfit mothers' based on their sexual orientation. Popular fears that children of lesbians will grow up to be homosexuals, or will have difficulty in their sex role orientation, or will be harmed in other ways by living with a lesbian mother, can be issues in child custody decisions made by the courts.

Resistance to claims of motherhood is especially likely for a co-mother who is not the biological parent of the child. Strategies to sustain an identity as mother under these conditions include second-parent adoption of the child, where that is a legally available option. In this way a legal bond is created between co-mother and child which legitimates claims to motherhood. Other legal steps to promote a co-mother's rights with the child include wills, guardianships, powers of attorney and a change in surname. These steps may be necessary, for example, before a co-mother's parents will invest time and other resources in their grandchild. They may also be necessary in order to protect a co-mother's relationship with the child in the event that the biological parent dies or if the partnership breaks up, which can be an issue in some relationships. Having a legal bond with a child in the absence of a biological relationship can also be essential for having authority over the child in dealing with schools or medical institutions if the biological mother is unavailable. Another strategy for maintaining an identity as a good mother is controlling expressions of intimacy so that lesbian identity is not revealed in situations where it might be contested. Lesbian mothers may decide to keep a low profile in order to avoid having their children socially stigmatized (Nations, 1997).

Being a lesbian, or being from a lesbian family, is a stigmatizing identity. On the other hand, being a mother is a legitimizing identity. Becoming a mother can therefore help lesbians to gain greater social acceptance than would otherwise be the case. Gillian Dunne reports from a study in England that strained or difficult relationships between some lesbians and their parents were transformed as daughters became mothers and their parents became grandparents (Dunne, 2000). In addition, many respondents reported experiencing high levels of enthusiastic support from heterosexual friends in their quest to become, and their experience of being, parents.

Dunne also reports that fathers featured in the lives of many of the English children born as a result of donor insemination. Like women in Sweden and Ireland (Ryan-Flood, 2005), most lesbian mothers who choose donor insemination prefer to have a known donor rather than an anonymous donor. Partly, no doubt, this may be because sperm bank facilities can be difficult or costly to access. However, the main reason appears to be social. Most lesbian mothers want their children to have the option of knowing who their fathers are, should they desire to do so. In some cases this extends to involving the father in interacting with the child so that children can normalize their family arrangements by being able to talk to their friends about activities with their father. Roisin Ryan-Flood reports that Swedish lesbians are far more likely to choose an involved donor than their Irish counterparts. They considered this to be important to enable the father to act as a male role model for the child. Although Swedish lesbian parents occasionally expressed misgivings about the complexities of negotiating parenting with a donor, the overall advantages were seen to outweigh any difficulties. On the whole, Swedish lesbian parents were comfortable with negotiating a mutually amicable degree of involvement on the part of donors. In Ireland, in contrast, the most common situation is for lesbians who become mothers through donor insemination to choose uninvolved donors whose identity remains a secret to the child. However, there is usually an understanding here that if a child becomes curious about the donor at a later date then he can be contacted by the child.

In England, Ireland and Sweden the majority of donors for lesbian mothers are gay men. According to Gillian Dunne, English lesbian parents prefer gay donors for three reasons (Dunne, 2000). First, they perceive gay men as presenting more acceptable and positive forms of masculinity since the dominant models of masculinity are felt to be unfavourable. Gay men who are involved donors are thought to be less likely to engage in sexist behaviour and therefore they are more likely to provide a positive role model for children. Second, lesbian mothers believe that gay donors are less likely to renege on agreements. And third, they are afraid that heterosexual donors might be more successful if they decided to challenge arrangements in relation to access and custody.

This was also a concern of Irish lesbian parents in the study by Roisin Ryan-Flood (Ryan-Flood, 2005). Irish respondents were concerned that a heterosexual donor might become too interested in the child and have a legal advantage in a custody case due to his conventional sexuality. In contrast, Swedish respondents, who were more likely to want involved donors, were concerned that heterosexual donors might lose interest in the child when they had other children. Lesbian parents in both countries were in favour of gay donors because they had a shared experience of homophobic oppression, and therefore had a sympathetic understanding of the complexities of choosing to parent within an openly lesbian lifestyle.

The family lives of lesbian parents are complex. So, too, are the lives of women who work in the sex trade. Maintaining relationships with men in the face of multiple sex partners is a challenge.

SEX AND INTIMACY

One of the criteria of intimacy in marriage and marriage-like relationships is exclusive sexual access to a partner. Sexual exclusivity and trust are highly valued in most intimate relationships in Western societies. For this reason a sense of intimacy in a close relationship can be difficult to reconcile with the practice of being sexually available to many partners. This can be a special problem for women who work in the sex trade. Some of these women develop an ability to switch on and off from work mode to home mode, but few are comfortable about telling friends or family about their work.

In a qualitative study of female sex workers in Melbourne, Australia, Warr and Pyett have examined the women's attitudes towards private sexual relationships and the difficulties that are associated with sustaining such relationships while engaging in sex work (Warr and Pyett, 1999). All the women in this study reported tensions associated with having a private sexual relationship while engaging in sex work. Those who were in such relationships reported that their partners felt uneasy about their sex work and were often jealous of their clients. Some women considered sex work and private relationships to be so incompatible that private sexual relationships were not viable. The problem here is that sex work simulates the romantic love that is expressed in a private relationship. Because of the nature of their work, these women could not express love and commitment through sexual exclusivity. They therefore made a deliberate decision to refrain from seeking love or intimacy until their circumstances changed.

Most of the women who were involved in private relationships felt that their sex work entailed a number of serious difficulties for their relationships. For example, their partners did not like them to talk about their work. As a result, these women were unable to discuss everyday issues at work as other women in relationships can do. Also, there were emotional difficulties in having sex with a partner after having sex at work. One way of handling this was to make a distinction between the types of sexual intimacy involved. Certain sexual acts, such as kissing, fondling or other shows of affection were privatized and were excluded from the range of sexual services offered for sale to clients. For all these women, condom use carried very strong associations with work, while not using condoms signified private sex. Condoms represented a barrier between themselves and their clients, and only sex without condoms felt like real sex. Unlike the views of other women, these women did not see working in the sex industry and being in an intimate relationship as deeply incompatible. Yet, they had to work at maintaining the sentiments that they attached to their private relationships. These relationships had to be constructed within the constraints of particular economic activities, and their meanings had to be defined in opposition to the meanings of their work.

Women who work in the sex trade have difficulty constructing intimate relationships because of the nature of the work that they do. Another challenge they face is the risk of infection with sexually transmitted diseases. HIV/AIDS is one such disease, which can have profound implications for family life.

AIDS AND FAMILY STRUCTURE

In some parts of the world, notably in Sub-Saharan Africa, AIDS has become a scourge which has impacted upon family structure. South Africa, for example, is one country in which the impact of the HIV/AIDS epidemic has been most noticeable. AIDS is an incurable disease that usually leads to death, and it therefore causes increased mortality. Many of those who are affected are relatively young, and in their childbearing and child-rearing years. In 2000, AIDS accounted for about 20 per cent of all adult deaths, and approximately 40 per cent of the deaths of adults aged 15–49 years in South Africa (Sekokotla and Mturi, 2004). The majority of people who die from AIDS are in their reproductive years and are often parents. Because of its impact on parents, the increased mortality associated with AIDS has resulted in a growing number of orphans in need of care. The consequence of this is changes in living patterns at the individual and family levels.

Traditionally, orphans were cared for by the safety net of the extended family. Aunts, uncles and grandparents have all been called on to look after children whose parents have died. In particular, grandparents, many of whom are elderly, have played an important role in caring for their orphaned grandchildren. A type of family structure created in this way is that which comprises grandmother and/or grandfather with their grandchildren. Sekokotla and Mturi refer to this type of family as the skip-generation family (Sekokotla and Mturi, 2004). However, sometimes grandparents are dead or too old to care for grandchildren, in which case the children may opt to stay alone at their parents' home.

Skip-generation families are not the only families created by the AIDS epidemic. That is because the extended family system is under increasing strain as relatives struggle to cope with the rising number of AIDS orphans. In some cases there is no adult available and the children are left to cope on their own. The result is that older children may have to look after their siblings in a new family structure that is headed by a child. Many of these child-headed families face major difficulties, including lack of money to meet basic needs such as food and clothing and to pay school fees, as well as lack of access to health care, and sometimes lack of shelter as a result of eviction from their parents' house. In order to provide for themselves, some of these children have to resort to crime, prostitution and selling drugs for survival.

DISCUSSION

In this chapter we have looked at various aspects of sexuality and their relation to family life. Sexual relations are an important form of family interaction, and they can also have implications for family structure. We began by discussing attitudes towards premarital sexuality. Generally, attitudes have become more permissive, though important cultural differences remain between different countries. In some places, majority opinion continues to be opposed to premarital sex, and it continues to excite social controversy. Also controversial are same-sex relationships, which were discussed next. Attention was focused on the experiences of lesbian mothers who must construct family life in opposition to the dominant assumptions about families. Next, we considered the challenges that women who work in the sex trade encounter when they seek to sustain intimate relationships in a context where they have multiple sexual partners. Finally, we considered the impact of AIDS on family structure. In some parts of the world this sexually transmitted disease has resulted in increased numbers of orphans who must be cared for in alternatives to the nuclear family.

References

Agree, E. M., Biddlecom, A. E. and Valente, T. W. (2005) 'Intergenerational Transfers of Resources between Older Persons and Extended Kin in Taiwan and the Philippines', *Population Studies*, 59 (2): 181–95.

Ahmed, P. and Emigh, R. J. (2005) 'Household Composition in Post-Socialist Eastern Europe', *International Journal of Sociology and Social Policy*, 25 (3): 9–41.

Aldous, J. (1995) 'New Views of Grandparents in Intergenerational Context', *Journal of Family Issues*, 16 (1): 104–22.

Amato, P. R., Loomis, L. S. and Booth, A. (1995) 'Parental Divorce, Marital Conflict, and Offspring Well-being during Early Adulthood', *Social Forces*, 73 (3): 895–915.

Aquilino, W. S. (1991) 'Family Structure and Home-Leaving: A Further Specification of the Relationship', *Journal of Marriage and the Family*, 53 (4): 999–1010.

Arber, S. and Ginn, J. (1990) 'The Meaning of Informal Care: Gender and the Contribution of Elderly People', *Ageing and Society*, 10 (4): 429–54.

Arber, S. and Ginn, J. (1995) 'Gender Differences in the Relationship between Paid Employment and Informal Care', *Work, Employment and Society*, 9 (3): 445–71.

Arnold, F., Choe, M. K. and Roy, T. K. (1998) 'Son Preference, the Family-Building Process and Child Mortality in India', *Population Studies*, 52 (3): 301–15.

Aronson, J. (1990) 'Women's Perspectives on Informal Care of the Elderly: Public Ideology and Personal Experience of Giving and Receiving Care', *Ageing and Society*, 10 (1): 61–84.

Bahr, H. M., Déchaux, J.-H. and Stiehr, K. (1994) 'The Changing Bonds of Kinship: Parents and Adult Children', in S. Langlois (ed.), *Convergence or Divergence?* Montreal and Kingston: McGill-Queen's University Press.

Beaujot, R. (1990) 'The Family and Demographic Change in Canada: Economic and Cultural Interpretations and Solutions', *Journal of Comparative Family Studies*, 21 (1): 25–38.

Berger, P., Berger, B. and Kellner, H. (1973) *The Homeless Mind*, New York: Random House.

Berger, P. and Kellner, H. (1964) 'Marriage and the Construction of Reality', *Diogenes*, 46: 1–24.

Bernardes, J. (1985) 'Do We Really Know What "The Family" Is?', in P. Close and R. Collins (eds), *Family and Economy in Modern Society*, Basingstoke: Macmillan.

Bernardes, J. (1999) 'We Must Not Define "The Family"!', *Marriage and Family Review*, 28 (3–4): 21–41.

Bernhardt, E., Gähler, M. and Goldscheider, F. (2005) 'Childhood Family Structure and Routes out of the Parental Home in Sweden', *Acta Sociologica*, 48 (2): 99–115.

Blossfeld, H.-P. and Huinink, J. (1991) 'Human Capital Investments or Norms of Role Transition? How Women's Schooling and Career Affect the Process of Family Formation', *American Journal of Sociology*, 97 (1): 143–68.

Blossfeld, H.-P., Klijzing, E., Pohl, K. and Rohwer, G. (1999) 'Why Do Cohabiting Couples Marry? An Example of a Causal Event History Approach to Interdependent Systems', *Quality and Quantity*, 33 (3): 229–42.

Blum, L. M. and Deussen, T. (1996) 'Negotiating Independent Motherhood: Working-Class African American Women Talk about Marriage and Motherhood', *Gender and Society*, 10 (2): 199–211.

Bock, J. D. (2000) 'Doing the Right Thing? Single Mothers by Choice and the Struggle for Legitimacy', *Gender and Society*, 14 (1): 62–86.

Brannen, J. and Moss, P. (1998) 'The Polarisation and Intensification of Parental Employment in Britain: Consequences for Children, Families and the Community', *Community, Work and Family*, 1 (3): 229–47.

Breines, W. and Gordon, L. (1983) 'The New Scholarship on Family Violence', *Signs*, 8 (3): 490–531.

Brooks-Gunn, J. and Duncan, G. J. (1997) 'The Effects of Poverty on Children', *The Future of Children*, 7 (2): 55–71.

Büchner, P., Krüger, H.-H. and du Bois Reymond, M. (1994) 'Growing Up as a "Modern" Child in Western Europe: The Impact of Modernization and Civilization Processes on the Everyday Lives of Children', *Sociological Studies of Children*, 6: 1–23.

Bumpass, L. L., Sweet, J. A. and Cherlin, A. (1991) 'The Role of Cohabitation in Declining Rates of Marriage', *Journal of Marriage and the Family*, 53 (4): 913–27.

Caldwell, G., Stiehr, K., Modell, J. and Del Campo, S. (1994) 'Differing Levels of Low Fertility', in S. Langlois (ed.), *Convergence or Divergence?* Montreal and Kingston: McGill-Queen's University Press.

Caldwell, J. C. (1976) 'Toward a Restatement of Demographic Transition Theory', *Population and Development Review*, 2 (3/4): 321–66.

Caldwell, J. C. (1978) 'A Theory of Fertility: From High Plateau to Destabilization', *Population and Development Review*, 4 (4): 553–73.

Chafetz, J. S. and Hagan, J. (1996) 'The Gender Division of Labor and Family Change in Industrial Societies: A Theoretical Accounting', *Journal of Comparative Family Studies*, 27 (2): 187–219.

Cheal, D. (1987) ' "Showing Them You Love Them": Gift Giving and the Dialectic of Intimacy', *The Sociological Review*, 35 (1): 151–69.

Chen, F. (2005) 'Residential Patterns of Parents and their Married Children in Contemporary China: A Life Course Approach', *Population Research and Policy Review*, 24 (2): 125–48.

Cherlin, A. J. (1999) 'Going to Extremes: Family Structure, Children's Well-being, and Social Science', *Demography*, 36 (4): 421–8.

Chesnais, J.-C. (1996) 'Fertility, Family, and Social Policy in Contemporary Western Europe', *Population and Development Review* 22 (4): 729–39.

Choe, M. K., Hongsheng, H. and Feng, W. (1995) 'Effects of Gender, Birth Order, and other Correlates on Childhood Mortality in China', *Social Biology*, 42 (1–2): 50–64.

Choi, S.-J. (1996) 'The Family and Ageing in Korea: A New Concern and Challenge', *Ageing and Society*, 16 (1): 1–25.

Chowdhury, F. I. and Trovato, F. (1994) 'The Role and Status of Women and the Timing of Marriage in Five Asian Countries', *Journal of Comparative Family Studies*, 25 (2): 143–57.

Christopher, F. S. and Sprecher, S. (2000) 'Sexuality in Marriage, Dating, and other Relationships: A Decade Review', *Journal of Marriage and the Family*, 62 (4): 999–1017.

Clark, W. and Crompton, S. (2006) 'Till Death Do Us Part? The Risk of First and Second Marriage Dissolution', *Canadian Social Trends*, 81: 23–33.

Cleland, A. and Tisdall, K. (2005) 'The Challenge of Antisocial Behaviour: New Relationships between the State, Children and Parents', *International Journal of Law, Policy and the Family*, 19 (3): 395–420.

Coles, B. (1995) *Youth and Social Policy*, London: UCL Press.

Curran, S. R., McLanahan, S. and Knab, J. (2003) 'Does Remarriage Expand Perceptions of Kinship Support among the Elderly?', *Social Science Research*, 32 (2): 171–90.

Desai, S. (1992) 'Children at Risk: The Role of Family Structure in Latin America and West Africa', *Population and Development Review*, 18 (4): 689–717.

Devereaux, M. S. (1993) 'Time Use of Canadians in 1992', *Canadian Social Trends*, 30: 13–16.

Drobnic, S. (2000) 'The Effects of Children on Married and Lone Mothers' Employment in the United States and (West) Germany', *European Sociological Review*, 16 (2): 137–57.

Drobnic, S., Blossfeld, H.-P. and Rohwer, G. (1999) 'Dynamics of Women's Employment Patterns over the Family Life Course: A Comparison of the United States and Germany', *Journal of Marriage and the Family*, 61 (1): 133–46.

Dronkers, J. (1994) 'The Changing Effects of Lone Parent Families on the Educational Attainment of their Children in a European Welfare State', *Sociology*, 28 (1): 171–91.

Du Bois-Reymond, M. (1995) 'The Role of Parents in the Transition Period of Young People', in M. du Bois-Reymond, R. Diekstra, K. Hurrelmann and E. Peters (eds), *Childhood and Youth in Germany and the Netherlands*, Berlin: Walter de Gruyter.

Duncan, G. J. (1996) 'Income Dynamics and Health', *International Journal of Health Services*, 26 (3): 419–44.

Duncan, G. J., Yeung, W. J., Brooks-Gunn, J. and Smith, J. R. (1998) 'How Much Does Childhood Poverty Affect the Life Chances of Children?', *American Sociological Review*, 63 (3): 406–23.

Dunne, G. A. (2000) 'Opting into Motherhood: Lesbians Blurring the Boundaries and Transforming the Meaning of Parenthood and Kinship', *Gender and Society*, 14 (1): 11–35.

Edgar, D. and Glezer, H. (1994) 'Family and Intimacy: Family Careers and the Reconstruction of Private Life', *International Social Science Journal*, 139: 117–39.

Eichler, M. (1981) 'The Inadequacy of the Monolithic Model of the Family', *Canadian Journal of Sociology*, 6 (3): 367–88.

Elmelech, Y. (2005) 'Attitudes toward Familial Obligation in the United States and in Japan', *Sociological Inquiry*, 75 (4): 497–526.

Ermisch, J. and Francesconi, M. (1998) 'Cohabitation in Great Britain: Not for Long, but Here to Stay', *Working Papers of the ESRC Research Centre on Micro-social Change*, Paper 98-1, Colchester: University of Essex.

Evandrou, M. and Glaser, K. (2003) 'Combining Work and Family Life: The Pension Penalty of Caring', *Ageing and Society*, 23 (5): 583–601.

Ezawa, A. and Fujiwara, C. (2005) 'Lone Mothers and Welfare-to-Work Policies in Japan and the United States: Towards an Alternative Perspective', *Journal of Sociology and Social Welfare*, 32 (4): 41–63.

Featherstone, B. (2006) 'Rethinking Family Support in the Current Policy Context', *British Journal of Social Work*, 36 (1): 5–19.

Ferree, M. M. (1990) 'Beyond Separate Spheres: Feminism and Family Research', *Journal of Marriage and the Family*, 52 (4): 866–84.

Ferree, M. M. (1991a) 'Gender, Conflict and Change: Family Roles in Biographical Perspective', in W. Heinz (ed.), *Theoretical Advances in Life Course Research*, Weinheim: Deutscher Studien Verlag.

Ferree, M.M. (1991b) 'The Gender Division of Labor in Two-Earner Marriages: Dimensions of Variability and Change', *Journal of Family Issues*, 12 (2): 158–80.

Finch, J. (1995) 'Responsibilities, Obligations and Commitments', in I. Allen and E. Perkins (eds), *The Future of Family Care for Older People*, London: HMSO.

Finch, J. and Mason, J. (1990a) 'Filial Obligations and Kin Support for Elderly People', *Ageing and Society*, 10 (2): 151–75.

Finch, J. and Mason, J. (1990b) 'Divorce, Remarriage and Family Obligations', *Sociological Review*, 38 (2): 219–46.

Finch, J. and Mason, J. (1990c) 'Gender, Employment and Responsibilities to Kin', *Work, Employment and Society*, 4 (3): 349–67.

Frønes, I. (1997) 'The Transformation of Childhood: Children and Families in Postwar Norway', *Acta Sociologica*, 40 (1): 17–30.

Fu, X. (1996) 'A Macro-level Longitudinal Analysis of Marriage and Divorce Rates: The Effects of Modernization and Religious Affiliation', *Family Perspective*, 30 (2): 103–30.

Furstenberg, F. F. (1994) 'History and Current Status of Divorce in the United States', *The Future of Children*, 4 (1): 29–43.

Gelles, R. J. (1977) 'Power, Sex, and Violence: The Case of Marital Rape', *The Family Coordinator*, 26 (4): 339–47.

George, A. (1998) 'Differential Perspectives of Men and Women in Mumbai, India on Sexual Relations within Marriage', *Reproductive Health Matters*, 6 (12): 87–96.

George, S. and Dickerson, B. J. (1995) 'The Role of the Grandmother in Poor Single-Mother Families and Households', in B. J. Dickerson (ed.), *African American Single Mothers: Understanding their Lives and Families*, Thousand Oaks: Sage Publications.

Gershuny, J. (1992) 'Change in the Domestic Division of Labour in the UK, 1975–1987: Dependent Labour versus Adaptive Partnership', in N. Abercrombie and A. Warde (eds), *Social Change in Contemporary Britain*, Cambridge: Polity Press.

Gerson, K. (1991) 'Coping with Commitment: Dilemmas and Conflicts of Family Life', in A. Wolfe (ed.), *America at Century's End*, Berkeley: University of California Press.

Gerson, K. (1994) 'A Few Good Men: Overcoming the Barriers to Involved Fatherhood', *American Prospect*, 16 (Winter): 78–90.

Gerson, K. (1997) 'The Social Construction of Fatherhood', in T. Arendell (ed.), *Contemporary Parenting*, Thousand Oaks: Sage.

Ghuman, S. (2005) 'Attitudes about Sex and Marital Sexual Behavior in Hai Duong Province, Vietnam', *Studies in Family Planning*, 36 (2): 95–106.

Giddens, A. (1991) *Modernity and Self-Identity: Self and Society in the Late Modern Age*, Stanford: Stanford University Press.

Gillis, J. R. (1989) 'Ritualization of Middle-Class Family Life in Nineteenth Century Britain', *International Journal of Politics, Culture, and Society*, 3 (2): 213–35.

Glenn, E. N. (1987) 'Gender and the Family', in B. B. Hess and M. M. Ferree (eds), *Analyzing Gender*, Newbury Park: Sage.

Glezer, H. (1993) 'Pathways to Family Formation: To Tie or Not to Tie the Knot?', *Family Matters*, 34 (May): 16–20.

Gross, H. E. (1980) 'Couples Who Live Apart: Time/Place Disjunctions and Their Consequences', *Symbolic Interaction*, 3 (Fall): 69–82.

Grundy, E. (2005) 'Reciprocity in Relationships: Socio-economic and Health Influences on Intergenerational Exchanges between Third Age Parents and their Adult Children in Great Britain', *British Journal of Sociology*, 56 (2): 233–55.

Gubrium, J. F. (1987) 'Organizational Embeddedness and Family Life', in T. H. Brubaker (ed.), *Aging, Health, and Family*, Newbury Park: Sage.

Gubrium, J. F. and Lynott, R. J. (1985) 'Family Rhetoric as Social Order', *Journal of Family Issues*, 6 (1): 129–51.

Guest, P. (1992) 'Marital Dissolution and Development in Indonesia', *Journal of Comparative Family Studies*, 23 (1): 95–113.

Ha, J.-H., Carr, D., Utz, R. and Nesse, R. (2006) 'Older Adult's Perceptions of Intergenerational Support after Widowhood: How Do Men and Women Differ?', *Journal of Family Issues*, 27 (1): 3–30.

Haas, L. (1999) 'Families and Work', in M. Sussman, S. Steinmetz and

G. Peterson (eds), *Handbook of Marriage and the Family*, 2nd edn, New York: Plenum.

Haj-Yahia, M. M. (1998) 'A Patriarchal Perspective of Beliefs about Wife Beating among Palestinian Men from the West Bank and the Gaza Strip', *Journal of Family Issues*, 19 (5): 595–621.

Hall, D. R. (1996) 'Marriage as a Pure Relationship: Exploring the Link between Premarital Cohabitation and Divorce in Canada', *Journal of Comparative Family Studies*, 27 (1): 1–12.

Hanson, T. L., McLanahan, S. S. and Thomson, E. (1998) 'Windows on Divorce: Before and After', *Social Science Research*, 27 (3): 329–49.

Hareven, T. K. (1977) 'Family Time and Historical Time', *Daedalus*, (Spring): 57–70.

Hareven, T. K. (1991) 'The Home and the Family in Historical Perspective', *Social Research*, 58 (1): 253–85.

Harrop, A. and Moss, P. (1995) 'Trends in Parental Employment', *Work, Employment and Society*, 9 (3): 421–44.

Hartmann, H. I. (1981) 'The Family as the Locus of Gender, Class, and Political Struggle: The Example of Housework', *Signs*, 6 (3): 366–94.

Hashimoto, A. (1996) *The Gift of Generations: Japanese and American Perspectives on Aging and the Social Contract*, Cambridge: Cambridge University Press.

Hashimoto, R. and Takahashi, M. (1995) 'Between Family Obligation and Social Care: The Significance of Institutional Care for the Elderly in Japan', *Journal of Sociology and Social Welfare*, 22 (4): 47–67.

Hays, S. (1996) *The Cultural Contradictions of Motherhood*, New Haven: Yale University Press.

Heaton, T. B. (1996) 'Socioeconomic and Familial Status of Women Associated with Age at First Marriage in Three Islamic Societies', *Journal of Comparative Family Studies*, 27 (1): 41–58.

Heaton, T. B., Cammack, M. and Young, L. (2001) 'Why is the Divorce Rate Declining in Indonesia?', *Journal of Marriage and Family*, 63 (2): 480–90.

Hequembourg, A. L. and Farrell, M. P. (1999) 'Lesbian Motherhood: Negotiating Marginal-Mainstream Identities', *Gender and Society*, 13 (4): 540–57.

Hertz, R. (1999) 'Working to Place Family at the Center of Life: Dual-Earner and Single-Parent Strategies', *Annals of the American Academy of Political and Social Science*, 562: 16–31.

Hiilamo, H. (2004) 'Changing Family Policy in Sweden and Finland during the 1990s', *Social Policy and Administration*, 38 (1): 21–40.

Hill, M. S. (1995) 'When Is a Family a Family? Evidence from Survey Data and Implications for Family Policy', *Journal of Family and Economic Issues*, 16 (1): 35–64.

Højgaard, L. (1997) 'Working Fathers – Caught in the Web of the Symbolic Order of Gender', *Acta Sociologica*, 40 (3): 245–61.

Holstein, J. A. (1988) 'Studying "Family Usage": Family Image and Discourse in Mental Hospitalization Decisions', *Journal of Contemporary Ethnography*, 17 (3): 261–84.

Holstein, J. A. and Gubrium, J. (1999) 'What Is Family? Further Thoughts on a

Social Constructionist Approach', *Marriage and Family Review*, 28 (3–4): 3–20.

Jensen, A.-M. (1994) 'The Feminization of Childhood', in J. Qvortrup, M. Bardy, G. Sgritta and H. Wintersberger (eds), *Childhood Matters*, Aldershot: Avebury.

Jensen, A.-M. (1998) 'Parenthood and Childhood in the Scandinavian Countries: Challenges of Responsibility', *Childhood*, 5 (1): 55–67.

Johnson, C. L. (2000) 'Perspectives on American Kinship in the Later 1990s', *Journal of Marriage and the Family*, 62 (3): 623–39.

Jones, G. W. (1997) 'Modernization and Divorce: Contrasting Trends in Islamic Southeast Asia and the West', *Population and Development Review*, 23 (1): 95–114.

Jones, G. W., Asari, Y. and Djuartika, T. (1994) 'Divorce in West Java', *Journal of Comparative Family Studies*, 25 (3): 395–416.

Kamo, Y. (2000) 'Racial and Ethnic Differences in Extended Family Households', *Sociological Perspectives*, 43 (2): 211–29.

Karanja, W. W. (1994) 'The Phenomenon of "Outside Wives": Some Reflections on its Possible Influence on Fertility', in C. Bledsoe and G. Pison (eds), *Nuptiality in Sub-Saharan Africa*, Oxford: Clarendon Press.

Keating, N., Kerr, K., Warren, S., Grace, M. and Wertenberger, D. (1994) 'Who's the Family in Family Caregiving', *Canadian Journal on Aging*, 13 (2): 268–87.

Kemp, C. L. (2003) 'The Social and Demographic Contours of Contemporary Grandparenthood: Mapping Patterns in Canada and the United States', *Journal of Comparative Family Studies*, 34 (2): 187–212.

Kendall, L. (1996) *Getting Married in Korea: Of Gender, Morality, and Modernity*, Berkeley: University of California Press.

Kim, I. K. (1999) 'Population Aging in Korea: Social Problems and Solutions', *Journal of Sociology and Social Welfare*, 26 (1): 107–23.

Klett-Davies, M. (1997) 'Single Mothers in Germany', in S. Duncan and R. Edwards (eds), *Single Mothers in an International Context*, London: UCL Press.

Koyano, W. (1999) 'Population Aging, Changes in Living Arrangement, and the New Long-Term Care System in Japan', *Journal of Sociology and Social Welfare*, 26 (1): 155–67.

Kraaykamp, G. (2002) 'Trends and Countertrends in Sexual Permissiveness: Three Decades of Attitude Change in the Netherlands 1965–1995', *Journal of Marriage and Family*, 64 (1): 225–39.

Laslett, B. (1973) 'The Family as a Public and Private Institution', *Journal of Marriage and the Family*, 35: 480–92.

Lee, M. S. (1999) 'Kinship Structure and Behaviors of Kin-Relatives in Modern Korea', in S. L. Browning and R. R. Miller (eds), *Till Death Do Us Part: A Multicultural Anthology on Marriage*, Stamford, CT: JAI Press.

Leira, A. (1993) 'Mothers, Markets and the State: A Scandinavian "Model"?', *Journal of Social Policy*, 22 (3): 329–47.

Leira, A. (1994) 'Concepts of Caring: Loving, Thinking, and Doing', *Social Service Review*, 68 (2): 185–201.

Lewis, J. and Meredith, B. (1988) 'Daughters Caring for Mothers: the Experience of Caring and its Implications for Professional Helpers', *Ageing and Society*, 8 (1): 1–21.

Lin, I.-F., Goldman, N., Weinstein, M., Lin, Y.-H., Gorrindo, T. and Seeman, T. (2003) 'Gender Differences in Adult Children's Support of their Parents in Taiwan', *Journal of Marriage and Family*, 65 (1): 184–200.

Lind, A. (2004) 'Legislating the Family: Heterosexist Bias in Social Welfare Policy Frameworks', *Journal of Sociology and Social Welfare*, 31 (4): 21–35.

Lister, R. (2006) 'Children (but Not Women) First: New Labour, Child Welfare and Gender', *Critical Social Policy*, 26 (2): 315–35.

Litwak, E. (1960) 'Occupational Mobility and Extended Family Cohesion', *American Sociological Review*, 25 (February): 9–21.

Locoh, T. (1994) 'Social Change and Marriage Arrangements: New Types of Union in Lomé, Togo', in C. Bledsoe and G. Pison (eds), *Nuptiality in Sub-Saharan Africa*, Oxford: Clarendon Press.

Lowenstein, A. and Daatland, S. O. (2006) 'Filial Norms and Family Support in a Comparative Cross-National Context: Evidence from the OASIS Study', *Ageing and Society*, 26 (2): 203–23.

Macura, M., Eggers, M. and Frejka, T. (1995) 'Demographic Change and Public Policy in Europe', in H. Moors and R. Palomba (eds), *Population, Family, and Welfare*, Oxford: Clarendon Press.

Marcil-Gratton, N. (1993) 'Growing up with a Single Parent, A Transitional Experience? Some Demographic Measurements', in J. Hudson and B. Galaway (eds), *Single Parent Families*, Toronto: Thompson Educational Publishing.

Marsh, R. M. and Hsu, C.-K. (1995) 'Changes in Norms and Behavior Concerning Extended Kin in Taipei, Taiwan, 1963–1991', *Journal of Comparative Family Studies*, 26 (3): 349–69.

McLanahan, S. S. (1994) 'The Consequences of Single Motherhood', *American Prospect*, 18 (Summer): 48–58.

Menaghan, E. G. and Parcel, T. L. (1990) 'Parental Employment and Family Life: Research in the 1980s', *Journal of Marriage and the Family*, 52 (4): 1079–98.

Mills, M. B. (1998) 'Gendered Encounters with Modernity: Labor Migrants and Marriage Choices in Contemporary Thailand', *Identities: Global Studies in Culture and Power*, 5 (3): 301–34.

Mitchell, B. A., Wister, A. V. and Burch, T. K. (1989) 'The Family Environment and Leaving the Parental Home', *Journal of Marriage and the Family*, 51 (3): 605–13.

Morioka, K. (1996) 'Generational Relations and their Changes as they Affect the Status of Older People in Japan', in T. K. Hareven (ed.), *Aging and Generational Relations*, New York: Aldine de Gruyter.

Murdock, G. P. (1960) *Social Structure*, New York: Macmillan.

Murphy, B., Schofield, H., Nankervis, J., Bloch, S., Herrman, H. and Singh, B. (1997) 'Women with Multiple Roles: The Emotional Impact of Caring for Ageing Parents', *Ageing and Society*, 17 (3): 277–91.

Murphy-Lawless, J. and McCarthy, J. (1999) 'Social Policy and Fertility Change in Ireland: The Push to Legislate in Favour of Women's Agency', *The European Journal of Women's Studies*, 6 (1): 69–96.

Nations, L. (1997) 'Lesbian Mothers: A Descriptive Study of a Distinctive Family Structure', *Journal of Gay and Lesbian Social Services*, 7 (1): 23–47.

Niranjan, S., Nair, S. and Roy, T. K. (2005) 'A Socio-demographic Analysis of the Size and Structure of the Family in India', *Journal of Comparative Family Studies*, 36 (4): 623–51.

Ogawa, N. and Retherford, R. D. (1997) 'Shifting Costs of Caring for the Elderly back to Families in Japan: Will it Work?', *Population and Development Review*, 23 (1): 59–94.

Onwuachi-Willig, A. (2005) 'The Return of the Ring: Welfare Reform's Marriage Cure as the Revival of Post-Bellum Control', *California Law Review*, 93 (6): 1647–96.

Ouattara, M., Sen, P. and Thomson, M. (1998) 'Forced Marriage, Forced Sex: The Perils of Childhood for Girls', *Gender and Development*, 6 (3): 27–33.

Palomba, R. and Moors, H. (1995) 'Attitudes towards Marriage, Children, and Population Policies in Europe', in H. Moors and R. Palomba (eds), *Population, Family, and Welfare*, Oxford: Clarendon Press.

Parrado, E. A. and Tienda, M. (1997) 'Women's Roles and Family Formation in Venezuela: New Forms of Consensual Unions?', *Social Biology*, 44 (1–2): 1–24.

Pebley, A. R. and Rudkin, L. L. (1999) 'Grandparents Caring for Grandchildren: What Do We Know?' *Journal of Family Issues*, 20 (2): 218–42.

Pilcher, J. (1999) *Women in Contemporary Britain*, London: Routledge.

Pitshandenge, I. N. A. (1994) 'Marriage Law in Sub-Saharan Africa', in C. Bledsoe and G. Pison (eds), *Nuptiality in Sub-Saharan Africa*, Oxford: Clarendon Press.

Prasad, D. (1994) 'Dowry-Related Violence: A Content Analysis of News in Selected Newspapers', *Journal of Comparative Family Studies*, 25 (1): 71–89.

Pyper, W. (2006) 'Balancing Career and Care', *Perspectives on Labour and Income*, 7 (11): 5–15.

Quddus, A. H. G. (1992) 'The Adjustment of Couples who Live Apart: The Case of Bangladesh', *Journal of Comparative Family Studies*, 23 (2): 285–94.

Richards, L. (1989) 'Family and Home Ownership in Australia: The Nexus of Ideologies', *Marriage and Family Review* 14 (1/2): 173–93.

Richter, K. (1996) 'Living Separately as a Child-Care Strategy: Implications for Women's Work and Family in Urban Thailand', *Journal of Marriage and the Family*, 58 (2): 327–39.

Robinson, J. and Godbey, G. (1997) *Time for Life: The Surprising Ways Americans Use their Time*, University Park: Pennsylvania State University Press.

Ruggles, S. (1994a) 'The Origins of African-American Family Structure', *American Sociological Review*, 59 (1): 136–51.

Ruggles, S. (1994b) 'The Transformation of American Family Structure', *The American Historical Review*, 99 (1): 103–28.

Ryan-Flood, R. (2005) 'Contested Heteronormativities: Discourses of Fatherhood among Lesbian Parents in Sweden and Ireland', *Sexualities*, 8 (2): 189–204.

Sandqvist, K. (1992) 'Sweden's Sex-Role Scheme and Commitment to Gender Equality', in S. Lewis, D. Izraeli and H. Hootsmans (eds), *Dual-Earner Families*, London: Sage.

Sarkisian, N., Gerena, M. and Gerstel, N. (2006) 'Extended Family Ties among Mexicans, Puerto Ricans, and Whites: Superintegration or Disintegration', *Family Relations*, 55 (3): 331–44.

Sarkisian, N. and Gerstel, N. (2004) 'Kin Support among Blacks and Whites: Race and Family Organization', *American Sociological Review*, 69 (6): 812–37.

Saunders, P. (1989) 'The Meaning of "Home" in Contemporary English Culture', *Housing Studies*, 4 (3): 177–92.

Saurel-Cubizolles, M.-J., Romito, P., Escribà-Agüir, V., Lelong, N., Pons, R. M. and Ancel, P.-Y. (1999) 'Returning to Work after Childbirth in France, Italy, and Spain', *European Sociological Review*, 15 (2): 179–94.

Scott, J. (1997) 'Changing Households in Britain: Do Families Still Matter?', *The Sociological Review*, 45 (4): 591–620.

Sekokotla, D. and Mturi, A. J. (2004) 'Effects of the HIV/AIDS Epidemic on the South African Families', *Loyola Journal of Social Sciences*, 18 (2): 189–211.

Shalhoub-Kevorkian, N. (1999) 'The Politics of Disclosing Female Sexual Abuse: A Case Study of Palestinian Society', *Child Abuse and Neglect*, 23 (12): 1275–93.

Smock, P.J. (1993) 'The Economic Costs of Marital Disruption for Young Women over the Past Two Decades', *Demography*, 30 (3): 353–71.

Solsona, M. (1998) 'The Second Demographic Transition from a Gender Perspective', *Innovation*, 11 (2): 211–25.

Sorensen, A. (1994) 'Women's Economic Risk and the Economic Position of Single Mothers', *European Sociological Review*, 10 (2): 173–88.

Sorensen, A. and McLanahan, S. (1987) 'Married Women's Economic Dependency, 1940–1980', *American Journal of Sociology*, 93 (3): 659–87.

South, S. J. and Spitze, G. (1994) 'Housework in Marital and Nonmarital Households', *American Sociological Review*, 59 (3): 327–47.

Stacey, J. (1990) *Brave New Families: Stories of Domestic Upheaval in Late Twentieth Century America*, New York: Basic Books.

Stacey, J. (1991) 'Backward toward the Postmodern Family: Reflections on Gender, Kinship, and Class in the Silicon Valley', in A. Wolfe (ed.), *America at Century's End*, Berkeley: University of California Press.

Stier, H. and Tienda, M. (1997) 'Spouses or Babies? Race, Poverty and Pathways to Family Formation in Urban America', *Ethnic and Racial Studies*, 20 (1): 91–122.

Sug-In, K. (1998) 'The Extended Family in Contemporary Korea: Changing Patterns of Co-residence', *Korea Journal*, 38 (3): 178–209.

Suh, M. K. (1994) 'Women, Ageing and the Family in Korea', *Australian Journal on Ageing*, 13 (4): 175–7.

Sung, K.-t. (2001) 'Family Support for the Elderly in Korea: Continuity, Change, Future Directions, and Cross-Cultural Concerns', *Journal of Aging and Social Policy*, 12 (4): 65–79.

Szinovacz, M. (1996) 'Living with Grandparents: Variations by Cohort, Race, and Family Structure', *International Journal of Sociology and Social Policy*, 16 (12): 89–123.

Takagi, E. and Silverstein, M. (2006) 'Intergenerational Coresidence of the Japanese Elderly: Are Cultural Norms Proactive or Reactive?', *Research on Aging*, 28 (4): 473–92.

Thorne, B. (1982) 'Feminist Rethinking of the Family: An Overview', in B. Thorne with M. Yalom (eds), *Rethinking the Family: Some Feminist Questions*, New York: Longman.

Tilly, C. and Albelda, R. (1994) 'Family Structure and Family Earnings: The Determinants of Earnings Differences among Family Types', *Industrial Relations*, 33 (2): 151–67.

Tisdall, E. K. M. (2006) 'Antisocial Behaviour Legislation Meets Children's Services: Challenging Perspectives on Children, Parents and the State', *Critical Social Policy*, 26 (1): 101–20.

Trost, J. (1978) 'A Renewed Social Institution: Non-marital Cohabitation', *Acta Sociologica*, 21 (4): 303–15.

Trzcinski, E. (2000) 'Family Policy in Germany: A Feminist Dilemma?', *Feminist Economics*, 6 (1): 21–44.

Van Berkel, M. and De Graaf, N. D. (1998) 'Married Women's Economic Dependency in the Netherlands, 1979–1991', *British Journal of Sociology*, 49 (1): 97–117.

Walker, A. (1999) 'Gender and Family Relationships', in M. Sussman, S. Steinmetz and G. Peterson (eds), *Handbook of Marriage and the Family*, 2nd edn, New York: Plenum.

Ward, C., Dale, A. and Joshi, H. (1996) 'Income Dependency within Couples', in L. Morris and E. S. Lyon (eds), *Gender Relations in Public and Private*, Basingstoke: Macmillan.

Warr, D. J. and Pyett, P. M. (1999) 'Difficult Relations: Sex Work, Love and Intimacy', *Sociology of Health and Illness*, 21 (3): 290–309.

Warren, T. (2003) 'Class- and Gender-Based Working Time? Time Poverty and the Division of Domestic Labour', *Sociology*, 37 (4): 733–51.

Wood, K. and Jewkes, R. (1997) 'Violence, Rape, and Sexual Coercion: Everyday Love in a South African Township', *Gender and Development*, 5 (2): 41–6.

Wu, Z. (2000) *Cohabitation: An Alternative Form of Family Living*, Don Mills: Oxford University Press.

Xu, X. (1998) 'Convergence or Divergence: The Transformation of Marriage Relationships in Urban America and Urban China', *Journal of Asian and African Studies*, 33 (2): 181–204.

Yamato, R. (2006) 'Changing Attitudes towards Elderly Dependence in Postwar Japan', *Current Sociology*, 54 (2): 273–91.

Yi, Z. (2002) 'A Demographic Analysis of Family Households in China, 1982–1995', *Journal of Comparative Family Studies*, 33 (1): 15–34.

Zaretsky, E. (1976) *Capitalism, The Family and Personal Life*, New York: Harper and Row.

Zhao, J. Z., Rajulton, F. and Ravanera, Z. R. (1995) 'Leaving Parental Homes in Canada: Effects of Family Structure, Gender, and Culture', *Canadian Journal of Sociology*, 20 (1): 31–50.

Index

Between Sex and Power

Family in the World 1900-2000

Göran Therborn

The institution of the family changed hugely during the course of the twentieth century. In this major new work, Göran Therborn provides a global history and sociology of the family as an institution and of politics within the family, focusing on three dimensions of family relations: on the rights and powers of fathers and husbands; on marriage, cohabitation and extra-marital sexuality; and on population policy. Therborn's empirical analysis uses a multi-disciplinary approach to show how the major family systems of the world have been formed and developed. Therborn concludes by assessing what changes the family might see during the next century.

This book will be essential reading for anybody with an interest in either the sociology or the history of the family.

Contents

Routledge
Taylor & Francis Group

October 2004

PB: 978-0-415-30078-0 : **£28.99**
HB: 978-0-415-30077-3 : **£90.00**

Children, Place and Identity

Nation and Locality in Middle Childhood

Jonathan Scourfield, Cardiff University, UK
Bella Dicks, Cardiff University, UK
Mark Drakeford, Cardiff University, UK
Andrew Davies, Wavehill Consulting, UK

Children, Place
and Identity
Nation and locality in middle childhood

Jonathan Scourfield / Bella Dicks
Mark Drakeford / Andrew Davies

In this, the first sociology book to consider the important issue of how children identify with place and nation, the authors use original research and international case studies to explore this topic in depth. The book is rooted in original qualitative research the authors conducted with a diverse sample of children (aged eight to eleven) across Wales, but this data is also located in the context of existing international research on place identity.

The book features analysis of lively exchanges between children on their local, national and global identities, politics, language and race. It engages with important social and political questions such as whether cultural distinctiveness can be preserved in a context of globalization, whether we are destined to passively receive dominant representations of the nation or can creatively construct our own versions; and whether national identities are necessarily exclusive. Most importantly, the book focuses on what local and national identities mean to children in an era of cultural and economic globalization.

Including material on racialization, language, politics, class and gender, *Children, Place and Identity* will be a valuable resource to students and researchers of childhood studies and the sociology of childhood.

Contents

1. Childhoods, Places and Nations 2. Researching Children, Place and Identity 3. The Process of Children's National and Ethnic Identification 4. Global and National Dimensions of Place Identity 5. Local and Domestic Dimensions of Place Identity 6. Insiders and Outsiders 7. Ways of Speaking 8. Conclusion

2006

PB: 978-0-415-35127-0 : **£25.99**
HB: 978-0-415-35126-3 : **£80.00**

Routledge books are available from all good bookshops, or can be ordered by calling Taylor and Francis Direct Sales on +4401264343071 (credit card or-

Introducing the New Sexuality Studies

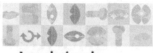

Original Essays and Interviews

Steven Seidma, State University of New York, USA
Nancy Fischer, Augsburg College, Minnesota, USA
Chet Meeks, Georgia State University, Atlanta, USA

Routledge
Taylor & Francis Group

Breaking new ground, both substantively and stylistically, this book offers students, academics and researchers an accessible, engaging introduction and overview of this emerging field. Its central premise is to explore the social character of sexuality, the role of social differences such as race or nationality in creating sexual variation, and the ways sex is entangled in relations of power and inequality. Through this novel approach the field of sexuality is therefore considered, for the first time, in multicultural, global, and comparative terms and from a truly social perspective.

This important volume consists of over fifty short and original essays on the key topics and themes in sexuality studies, and interviews with twelve leading scholars in the field which convey some of the most innovative work being done. Each contribution is original and conveys the latest thinking and research in writing that is clear and that uses examples to illustrate key points.

This topical and timely volume will be an invaluable resource to all those with an interest in sexuality studies.

Contents

2006

PB: 978-0-415-39900-5 : £25.99

Handbook of Youth and Young Adulthood

New Perspectives and Agendas

Andy Furlong

The parameters within which young people live their lives have changed radically. Changes in education and the labour market have led to an increased complexity of the youth phase and to an overall protraction in dependency and transitions. In a world where 'settled' occupational positions can prove elusive and where dependency stretches beyond traditional chronological boundaries, key terms like transition are losing their validity and even that a new phase of life between youth and adulthood (referred to as 'young adulthood' in Europe and 'emerging adulthood' in North America) is becoming established.

This handbook introduces up-to-date perspectives on a wide range of issues that affect and shape youth and young adulthood. It is based around ten inter-disciplinary themes and will introduce a new perspective on youth and adulthood. Contributors, established academics in the field, will provide an authoritative and multi-disciplinary overview of a field of study that offers unique insight on social change in advanced societies.

Each chapter will be an original contribution focusing on an area of contemporary theoretical and/or empirical significance. Each of the ten sections covers an important area of research - from education and the labour market to youth cultures, health and crime - discussing change and continuity in the lives of young people, introducing readers to some of the most important work in the field while highlighting the underlying perspectives that have been used to understand the complexity of modern youth and young adulthood.

Routledge
Taylor & Francis Group

October 2009

PB: 978-0-415-44541-2 : **£28.99**
HB: 978-0-415-44540-5 : **£95.00**

Routledge books are available from all good bookshops, or can be ordered by calling Taylor and Francis Direct Sales on +4401264343071 (credit card orders)